The Crimean War

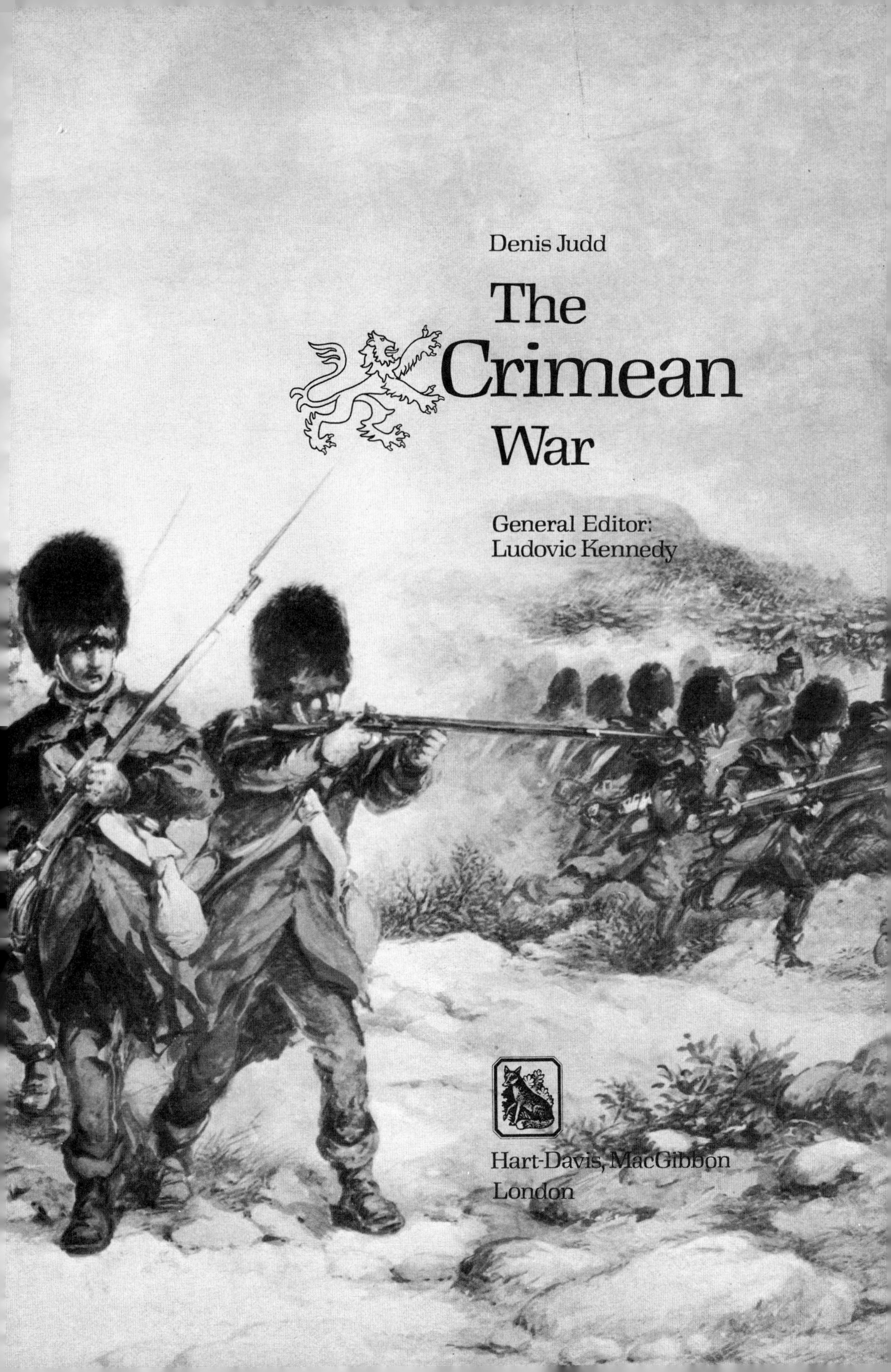

Denis Judd

The Crimean War

General Editor:
Ludovic Kennedy

Hart-Davis, MacGibbon
London

To Luke

Granada Publishing Limited
First published in Great Britain 1975 by
Hart-Davis, MacGibbon Ltd
Frogmore, St Albans, Hertfordshire, AL2 2NF and
3 Upper James Street, London W1R 4BP

ISBN 0 246 10804 5

Printed in Great Britain by
William Clowes & Sons, Limited
London, Beccles and Colchester

Contents

Acknowledgements

The photographs and illustrations in this book are reproduced by kind permission of the following. Those on pages 100 and 183 by the gracious permission of H.M. the Queen; pages 12, 15, 16, 20, 25, 26, 29, 35, 52, 68, 70, 73, 80, 92, 97, 103, 107, 109, 112, 115, 116, 127, 128–9, 132, 134, 139, 140, 142–3, 148, 150–51, 156, 160, 162, 172–3, 175, 176 and 178, National Army Museum; pages 8, 39 and 165, National Portrait Gallery; pages 24, 32, 46–7, 54–5, 56–7, 145, 167, 168–9 and 171, National Maritime Museum; pages 22, 44 and 48, Imperial War Museum; pages 18, 138 and 152–3, Novositi Press Agency; pages 41, 63, 67, 118–19, 149, 158–9 and 180, Victoria and Albert Museum; pages 87, 88–9, 90, 122–3 and 136, Mansell Collection; pages 72, 121 and 182, Trustees of the British Museum; page 11, By courtesy of Lauros-Giraudon and Versailles; page 23, Roger Viollet and Bibliotheque Nationale; page 30, The Science Museum; page 50, Royal Highland Fusiliers; pages 60–61, Royal Green Jackets; pages 74–5, By courtesy of Dewars; page 76, By courtesy of the Ministry of Defence, presented to the War Office by the 6th Earl of Lucan; page 76, City of Manchester Art Gallery; pages 98–9, Rifle Brigade Museum Trust; pages 104–5, Scots Guards Museum; page 125, By courtesy of the Curator of the RAMC Historical Museum, Aldershot; page 141, The Royal Leicestershire Regiment; pages 84, 144, 157 and 184, from Private Collections. Illustration Research Service supplied the pictures. The maps were drawn by Brian and Constance Dear.

Introduction

The Crimean War is today chiefly remembered for the Charge of the Light Brigade and for the achievements of Florence Nightingale. It was compounded of wasteful military muddles, by deeds of dashing heroism and by the sterling endurance of the common British soldier. Nor was the war a diplomatic failure from the British point of view, since Russian expansion was halted and the ailing Turkish Empire, 'the Sick Man of Europe', was propped up for several decades to come.

In many ways the Crimean War was a war of innovation, even though British officers fought in full dress uniforms, like gaudy dandies invited to a ball: the newly introduced rifle proved itself to be a formidable weapon; the electric telegraph linked the front line with London and Paris; W. H. Russell of *The Times* emerged as the first recognizable war correspondent, and Roger Fenton became the first war photographer.

Denis Judd in his compelling account of the Anglo-French campaigns against, as Palmerston belligerently put it, 'the Red-haired barbarians', describes with vivid insight the battles of the Alma, Balaclava and Inkerman, the terrible winter of 1854–5, the costly siege of Sebastopol, and the secondary campaigns fought in the key naval passages around Russia. From the substantial use of numerous eye-witness accounts of the conflict, a picture emerges of a war that, while it shook the Victorian belief in the efficiency and infallibility of its army, testified to its immense courage and unparalleled fortitude.

Ludovic Kennedy

Chapter 1

Origins of the War

The Crimean War of 1854–6 has become a byword for military incompetence mingled with administrative confusion. The stoical and heroic bearing of the common British soldier, and the misdirected but magnificent panache of the Light Brigade at Balaclava, are shrouded by recriminations that have obstinately survived the passage of one hundred and twenty years. The war broke the reputation, and possibly the will, of the British Commander-in-Chief, Lord Raglan, just as it besmirched the gaudy cavalry tunics of Lords Lucan and Cardigan. At the same time it brought the persistent and brazenly patriotic Lord Palmerston to his first premiership, and elevated one resilient and hard-working woman, Florence Nightingale, to immortality.

Oddly, it hardly deserves the title of the 'Crimean' War at all, since the Crimean peninsula was only one of three main theatres of the conflict, and fighting also took place on the lower Danube, and in Asia Minor to the foothills of the Caucasus mountains. At sea, naval action occurred not only in the Black Sea, but in the Sea of Azov, the White Sea, the Baltic, and on the Pacific coast of Russia. But for the British, whose commanders fumbled before Sebastopol and whose red-coated infantry died like flies of cholera and neglect from Calamita Bay to Balaclava, it has remained the Crimean War, and mid-Victorian terraces still bear the proud names of Inkerman Road or Alma Street or Raglan Court.

Britain entered the war with the object of thwarting Russian expansion in the Balkans and the Eastern Mediterranean, and especially to keep the great port of Constantinople out of Russian hands. In the half century before the outbreak of the Crimean War, Russia had doubled the size of her empire in Europe, and had advanced nearly a thousand miles into Central Asia where by the 1850s Tsarist regiments were actually nearer to Lahore and Delhi than to St Petersburg. But British interests in India were equally threatened by the prospect of Russian control of the Eastern Mediterranean and of the short overland route to the East.

Opposite Lord Palmerston, who became Prime Minister for the first time in February 1855 in order to win the war, by F. Cruikshank.

As long as the Ottoman empire was able to maintain its integrity, however, Russian ambitions could be contained. British statesmen were quite content to have the crescent moon fluttering over Constantinople, but to see it replaced by the Tsarist eagle was another matter. Unfortunately for British policymakers Turkish authority had become demonstrably enfeebled during the first half of the nineteenth century. In 1827 Britain had herself contributed to this decline when the Royal Navy, together with warships from France and Russia, had annihilated the Turkish fleet at Navarino, thus paving the way for Greece and the Danubian provinces of Moldavia and Wallachia to assert their independence from Ottoman rule. But this was not all. The Turkish Sultan was quite unable to bring to heel the rebellious Viceroy of Egypt, Mehemet Ali, whose campaigns of personal and dynastic aggrandisement caused considerable discomfort to the great powers of Europe during the 1830s. In the last resort, however, the European powers were prepared to intervene on Turkey's behalf against Mehemet Ali.

The task of propping up Turkish power was unlikely to remain congenial for an indefinite period of time. In particular, Russia regarded the prospect of the disintegration of the Turkish Empire with relish. The expansionist Tsar Nicholas I had already expressed his diagnosis of the situation, and his remedy, when he told the British ambassador in St Petersburg that 'We have on our hands a sick man – a very sick man; it will be a great misfortune if one of these days he should slip away from us, especially before all necessary arrangements have been made.' Britain, however, declined to help carve up 'the sick man' of Europe – the Turkish Empire.

In 1850 Russia reasserted her claim to protect the interests of the fifteen million or so Greek Orthodox citizens of the Turkish Empire. There was nothing novel in this, since Russia had on earlier occasions claimed to be the champion of the Orthodox Christians, thus hoping to maintain a tangible interest in the affairs of the Ottoman government. But in 1850 Russia did not have the field to herself. Prince Louis Napoleon, nephew of the great Bonaparte, had come to power in France and was soon to proclaim himself the Emperor Napoleon III. Finding the autocratic deportment of Nicholas I offensive, and seeking to assert the authority of his new regime, Louis Napoleon vigorously supported the claims of Roman Catholic orders in the Holy Land to the oversight of certain Christian shrines and holy places. There was, in particular, a bitter conflict between Orthodox and Catholic monks over the possession of the keys to the Church of the Holy Sepulchre in Bethlehem.

Opposite The Emperor Napoleon III, by Flandrin.

After a lengthy deliberation the Turkish Sultan decided the keys controversy in favour of the Catholic monks in December 1852. The Tsar immediately responded with a hair-raising exercise in brinkmanship. Early in 1853 he dispatched the arrogant and

Constantinople, by A. Cassagne.

bullying Prince Menshikov to Constantinople, where he was joined by the Russian admiral commanding the Black Sea Fleet and by the chief-of-staff of Russian forces on the Danube. Menshikov was charged with accomplishing two tasks: one was to maintain the exclusive privileges of Orthodox Christians in the Holy Places; the other was to insist on Russia's right to protect the Sultan's Christian subjects.

When Menshikov arrived in Constantinople, Turkish troops were in the process of suppressing a rebellion in Christian Montenegro. Menshikov proceeded to add to his list of demands by threatening the Sultan with war unless Turkish troops withdrew from Montenegro. The Sultan was inclined at first to surrender, but Lord Stratford de Redcliffe, the British ambassador at the Porte (the seat of Turkish government in Constantinople), encouraged him to reject Russia's demands. Menshikov left Constantinople in May 1853 believing that the Turks would change their minds. In order to aid this process, the Russian government announced that, unless they received the satisfaction they required, Imperial troops would occupy the Danubian provinces of Moldavia and Wallachia.

Britain and France now intervened in the dispute. On 15 June detachments of the British and French fleets were sent to the Dardanelles to sustain the Turks. In Vienna, the Austrians hastily summoned a conference of all interested parties in the hope of avoiding war, but a draft compromise formula backed by Britain, France and Russia was rejected by the Sultan. On 3 July 1853 the Tsar, having seen his ultimatum renewed and ignored, ordered his troops across the river Pruth and into Moldavia and Wallachia. Since Russia had the right, by treaty, to enter these provinces to preserve order, it was not inevitable that war would result from this move. Nor were the principalities part of Turkey proper, the Sultan merely exercising a nominal suzerainty over them. In Britain the Prime Minister, Lord Aberdeen, was disinclined to involve his government in a war, and in August 1853 the Queen's speech closing the Parliamentary session expressed the hope that peace would be maintained.

But the Turkish government was in fact prepared to resist the Russian challenge, and on 5 October 1853 formally declared war. The Porte's resolve was undoubtedly strengthened by the conviction that, in the last resort, Britain and France would intervene to prevent a crushing Russian victory. October saw the rival armies manoeuvring for tactical advantage along the lower Danube. Though the approach of winter limited the scope of the campaign to a series of indecisive clashes, it became evident that the Turkish commander, Omar Pasha, had achieved a considerable triumph by crossing the Danube (from the south) on a wide front. The Russians were determined to launch a great counter-offensive in the spring of 1854, driving across the Danube, to Silistria, and eventually towards the Bosphorus. But before this plan could be put into effect, Britain and France entered the war.

One of the incidents that drove Britain and France to the point of opening hostilities was the so-called 'massacre' of Sinope on 30 November 1853. Earlier in the month, the British and French fleets had violated the 1841 Straits Convention by sailing through the Dardanelles to the Sea of Marmara. There was a good deal of confusion over why the two fleets had acted as they did, but the British government robustly told Russia that the Royal Navy had moved at the request of a friendly power – the Turks. Within a few days a squadron of the Russian Black Sea Fleet attacked a Turkish squadron, commanded by Omar Pasha, at Sinope on the northern coast of Asia Minor.

Though both sides claimed that the other had fired first, the result was the annihilation of the seven Turkish frigates and two corvettes by superior Russian warships. In his contemporary

History of the War against Russia, E. H. Nolan claimed, with an indignation typical of many of his fellow-Britons, that 'never in naval warfare was so horrifying a slaughter before witnessed; five thousand sailors perished, the whole squadron was blown into one mass of broken and burning timber, and blasted and bleeding flesh. Yet amidst the floating timber, blackened and blood-stained, the Russian ships fired grape and canister, lest any of the wrecked should swim ashore.'

The horror expressed in the British and French press at the Sinope 'massacre' was to some extent unjustified – after all, Turkey and Russia were formally at war. But subsequently Britain and France moved more easily in step in their approach to the Turkish–Russian war. The French Emperor, Napoleon III, though not consistently belligerent, persuaded the British government to join with him in informing the Tsar that all Russian warships should return to the Crimean naval base of Sebastopol and that any further act of aggression against Turkey would be met by force. On 27 February a British and French joint note was sent to the Tsar demanding the withdrawal of Russian troops from Moldavia and Wallachia; the note was ignored and on 28 March Britain and France declared war on Russia.

Why did Britain and France go to war at this point? It was, after all, to be six months before the allies were able to mount an effective military challenge to Russia in the Crimea. In Britain, the Prime Minister, Lord Aberdeen, and many of his Cabinet had been determined to keep the country out of the Turkish–Russian conflict. John Bright and other Radical leaders had organised an effective Peace Society; *The Times* was unenthusiastic, and was vehemently described by a rival journal as 'The Russian organ of Printing House Square'; the Queen and Prince Albert were not war-mongers. Even in France the Emperor blew hot and cold: at one moment, he postured as the heir of the great Bonaparte, anxious both to advance the cause of European liberty and to revenge the catastrophe of the Russian campaign of 1812; at another, he declared *'L'Empire, c'est la paix.'*

But there were at the same time belligerent elements pushing Britain into open hostilities. Within the Cabinet, Lord Palmerston, from the unaccustomed and somewhat inappropriate post of Home Secretary, had for some time urged a belligerent policy against Russia. In this he had widespread support in Parliament and in the country. As a forthright yet flexible statesman, who had made his national reputation during his earlier lengthy tenure of the Foreign Office, Palmerston was considered by many to be in the wrong place at the wrong time in the months before the outbreak of war. Prince Albert indeed wrote to his confidant Baron Stockmar, 'the Palmerstonian stocks have gone up immensely, people saying that if he had been at the Foreign Office, he would by his energy have brought Russia to reason'. Certainly there is every reason to believe that Palmerston would have stood a good chance of averting war by his usual mixture of firmness and moderation. Since he was removed from the control of foreign affairs, however, his advice was more unyielding than it might otherwise have been, and he expressed a strong desire to 'make an Example of the Red-haired barbarians'.

After the Russian invasion of Moldavia and Wallachia in July 1853, Palmerston proceeded to promote anti-Russian feeling with all the means at his command; in the process he actively undermined the government's attempt to find a diplomatic solution to the situation. When in October 1853 Turkey declared war on

A Russian version of the naval 'massacre' of a Turkish squadron at Sinope, October 1853.

A satirical Russian view of the three allies, Britain, France and Turkey, couched in homely metaphor.

Russia, there was much popular enthusiasm in Britain; among those who rejoiced at the news were the Poet Laureate Alfred Tennyson, the writer Charles Kingsley, and the exiled Karl Marx. There were even voices in the streets that scurrilously sang of Prince Albert:

Little Al, the royal pal,
They say has turned a Russian

And a general dislike of foreign meddlers was expressed in the verse:

Bad luck, they say, both night and day,
To the Cobugs and the humbugs,
The Witermbugs and the Scarembugs,
And all the German horserugs;
And the old bug of Aberdeen,
The Peterbugs and Prussians.
May Providence protect the Turks
And massacre the Russians.

Lord Aberdeen thus found his government pushed inexorably towards war; pressure from the public, and from Parliament and

Cabinet ministers, was forcing his hand. Even so, he dallied as long as possible with diplomatic measures, which included the leisurely passing of notes between St Petersburg, London and Paris. At last accepting war as inevitable, the Prime Minister was determined to stay in power in order to limit Britain's military involvement and to make peace as soon as possible. Declaring that 'some fatal influence seems to have been at work', Aberdeen had to contemplate the bizarre prospect of Britain entering a war ostensibly to protect the European presence of the Ottoman Turks, and in alliance with the nephew of that Bonaparte whose long shadow had forty years before stretched ominously across the Channel.

Chapter 2

The Rival Armies

For almost a full year, from October 1853 to September 1854, the war on land was waged between Russia and Turkey, both on the Danube and in Asia Minor; the eventual Anglo-French invasion of the Crimean peninsula was a calculated counter-thrust designed to take pressure off the Turks in the other theatres of war and to capture and destroy the great Russian naval base of Sebastopol.

The Russian army which had precipitated the crisis with its menacing advance into the Danubian principalities was recruited from a nation accustomed to the repressive and regimented regime of the Tsar Nicholas I. The Russian population in the early 1850s was approximately eighty million; of these some four million were physically fit males of military age, and without exemption from service. In practice the Tsar maintained an army of three quarters of a million men, though by 1853 the total had risen to more than a million. The vast majority of these were illiterate peasants, ill-equipped for anything save a loyal and slavish obedience to the orders of their superiors. The Russian officers were for the most part equally unimpressive: many took their professional duties extremely lightly and pursued a vigorous and often dissolute social life when opportunity presented itself.

At the outbreak of the war the Russian army consisted of 188 infantry regiments, 32 rifle battalions and 48 frontier battalions (to garrison distant provinces of the Russian Empire). There were 56 cavalry regiments, 310 batteries of artillery, 11 battalions of engineers and 6 half battalions of bridging engineers. The elite of the army were the corps of the Imperial Guard and the corps of the Grenadiers. Quite a large number of the senior officers were of German origin, and one comparatively junior engineering officer of German stock, Franz Edward Ivanovitch Todleben, was to achieve undying fame as the organiser of the defences of Sebastopol.

In addition, there were the Cossacks. Only the Don Cossacks were liable for military service outside their own region, but the mobilisation of other Cossack tribes for internal duties meant that regular troops could be sent on foreign campaigns. The Cossacks were superb irregular cavalry, and of enormous value to the Russian high command for reconnaissance duties and in harrying (or keeping open) lines of supply and communication. Dressed in baggy trousers and tunics, and each armed with a pike, a carbine and a sword, the Cossacks, mounted on their hardy and fleet-footed ponies, enjoyed a fearsome reputation as savage and relentless foes.

Opposite Tsar Nicholas I, whose forceful and aggressive diplomacy led to the outbreak of the war, by Kruger.

A bivouac of Bashi-Bazouks – Turkish irregulars enjoying a fearsome reputation.

The theoretical strength of the Ottoman Empire's standing army in 1853 was about 700,000, recruited exclusively from those Muslims of military age. Following Sultan Mahmud II's destruction in 1826 of the elite corps of Janissaries (previously recruited largely from the Christian populations of Albania, Bosnia and Bulgaria), there had been an attempt to reorganise and reform the army and the navy: military schools had been opened, foreign instructors (many of them British) imported, and the conditions of service improved. This reforming initiative had not, however, transformed the Turkish forces into a fully modernised, well-equipped and adequately trained war-machine. Turkish troops continued to be badly paid and fitfully supplied; their officers possessed little technical knowledge and not much in the way of professional dedication and zest. Yet the rank and file soldier was loyal, stoical, and on the whole uncomplaining.

The Turkish infantry consisted of thirty-eight regiments, which, though poorly trained in the use of firearms, were dogged fighters at close quarters. The cavalry, even though reorganised on the model of their French counterparts, were also badly equipped and, on the whole, inefficiently led. There were 140 squadrons of Turkish cavalry, each nominally containing 143 horses, but in the event, they displayed neither sufficient dash nor solidity. Nor did the Turkish artillery inspire much confidence, composed as it was of batteries containing a motley collection of muzzle and breech-loaders, and smooth and rifled-bore cannon. There was also a corps of engineers, some two thousand in all, but their equipment and technical knowledge was generally not impressive.

Apart from the units of its regular army, the Turkish Empire could muster a colourful array of irregular troops. There were the Bashi-Bazouks, an ill-disciplined force recruited from the dregs of Turkish urban society and often proving to be more trouble than they were worth when campaigning started. Then there were Spahis and Bedouins, mostly embodied in irregular cavalry units under their own Arab leaders; ten thousand of them were raised during the Crimean War, but they were erratically led and frequently unreliable, and their main value lay in relieving regular troops of behind-the-lines activities. In theory, the Sultan could also call on contingents from countries nominally under his suzerainty – notably Egypt and Tunis. But the Khedive of Egypt, Abbas, was unwilling to subordinate his country to the Porte following the strenuous and ultimately successful efforts of his grandfather Mehemet Ali to achieve a considerable degree of independence from his overlord in Constantinople. Tunis was only able to provide a token force during the war.

The French forces that were dispatched to the Crimea were drawn from an army that was almost forty years removed from the great days of the first Napoleon. In the interim the splendid martial traditions based on the glories of Wagram, Austerlitz and Jena had survived undimmed, overshadowing the more uncomfortable memories of Leipzig and Waterloo. Nor had the French army been inactive since Waterloo: apart from forays into Spain, Italy and Belgium, Algeria had been conquered – thus providing valuable military experience for the forces needed to extend and maintain French rule in that province.

Overall the French army was the best equipped and the most professionally led of all the forces that fought in the Crimean War. While the democratic traditions of the Republican and Napoleonic wars had necessarily been diluted by the restoration of the Bourbons in 1815 and the Orleanist regime of King Louis Philippe (1830–48), promotion from the ranks was commonplace, and the officer class in general was less aristocratic and far more professional than its British equivalent. The coup d'état of Louis Napoleon in 1851 had, however, brought one military disadvantage in its wake; this was the advancement of senior officers who had either supported the

Prince Napoleon, a nephew of the great Bonaparte and cousin of the Emperor, and known as 'Plon-Plon'.

coup or were faithful servants of the newly established Emperor.

Of the senior French commanders who were dispatched to the Crimea most owed their position to their past loyalty to Napoleon III. The Commander-in-Chief of the French army was Marshal St Arnaud, fifty-three years old, and very experienced in the Algerian campaigns. He had been in charge of the 1851 military operations which had brought Louis Napoleon the imperial crown. He was an able enough soldier, but by 1854 stricken by the illness (cancer of the stomach) that was to cause his death in the Crimea before the end of the year.

The initial French expeditionary force consisted of four infantry divisions (of about ten thousand men each), with eight-and-a-half

Marshal St Arnaud, Commander-in-Chief of the French Army, by A. Maurin.

batteries of field artillery, and a cavalry detachment of Spahis or *Chasseurs d'Afrique*. The commander of the 1st Division was the forty-five-year-old General Canrobert (later nicknamed 'Bob can't' by the British troops); he had been Napoleon III's aide-de-camp during the 1851 coup, and had previously seen much service in North Africa. The 2nd Division was led by General Bosquet, aged forty-four, an artilleryman with North African experience. The 3rd Division was commanded by Prince Napoleon Joseph Bonaparte, the thirty-two-year-old cousin of the Emperor, and also his heir; he was a tall, fussy, ambitious man with a serious turn of mind but hardly any experience of active service; he was nicknamed 'Plon-Plon'. The commander of the 4th Division was

General Forey, who was fifty years of age and had seen considerable service in North Africa. The French divisional commanders were notably younger than their British equivalents, their average age being forty-two as opposed to fifty-five; in addition, they had all, with the exception of Prince Napoleon, acquired recent and quite extensive campaign experience.

But the most striking superiority of the French army over the British was in the matter of administrative organisation and supply. Drawing the obvious lesson from the Algerian campaigns that well-fed and properly equipped troops were able to fight with greater enthusiasm and confidence, the army was itself responsible for administering supply and welfare. Properly trained staff

Left The Anglo-French navies approach the Black Sea, January 1854.

Below General Canrobert, nicknamed 'Bob-can't' by the British troops.

ensured that the pay, rations, medical services and supply arrangements of the French soldiers were as lavish as possible, and efficiently administered. Once fighting began there were ten hospitals to cope with the wounded and the sick, a task accomplished without any of the horrifying confusion and neglect that characterised British medical care during the early part of the war. The British officers and men were quick to make unfavourable and envious comparisons between their own equipment and supplies and those of their allies, and in the early days of the war one British officer remarked that apparently the French had come to colonise rather than conquer.

The British army that sailed for the Crimea was proudly des-

British Infantry piling arms.

cribed by *The Times* as 'the finest army that has ever left these shores'. But the dashing appearance of the cavalry brigades, the spick and span uniforms of the regiments of infantry, only served to camouflage the problems and inadequacies in the command and organisation of the army. Given the disgraceful neglect of the British army since the ending of the Napoleonic Wars, probably only divine intervention could have averted the exhibition of chaos and indecisiveness in the Crimea. Not that the years between 1815 and 1854 had been barren of British triumphs, as a variety of campaigns in India, Southern Africa and New Zealand showed. But these victories had been achieved against non-European forces. Moreover in India the troops raised by the East India Company (both British and sepoy) had borne the brunt of the fighting. In 1854 the British faced neither Kaffirs nor Baluchis, but Russian forces that had recently plunged aggressively into Moldavia and Wallachia, had destroyed the Turkish fleet at Sinope in November 1853, and whose immediate forbears had ripped the heart out of Napoleon's armies in 1812–13. Furthermore the Russian rank and file, though they suffered worse conditions of service than their British counterparts, were fighting for the fatherland *in* the fatherland and could be counted on to resist ferociously.

The British forces that were dispatched to the Crimea in April 1854 were composed of five infantry divisions and one cavalry division. The common foot soldier was poorly paid (receiving a shilling a day, plus a penny a day beer money), fed on monotonous rations consisting mostly of beef broth and potatoes, ferociously disciplined, and packed into a fancy uniform that was well suited to the parade ground but was expected to be equally serviceable in tundra, veld and equatorial rain forest. The British infantry were mostly equipped with the extremely effective Minié rifle, which was replacing the famous 'Brown Bess' muzzle-loader. The Minié rifle was not exclusive to the British; their French allies had it, and so did some of their Russian opponents. In any case, the chief tactic employed on the battlefield was to manoeuvre to within range of the enemy, unleash a volley (or two if you were lucky) and then close in for hand-to-hand fighting. In these circumstances, the quality of firearm employed was of marginal importance, and the making use of cover generally scorned.

In a stand-up fight the quality of tactical military leadership was as important as the endurance and obedience of the rank and file. There were enough recent examples of the British soldier's courage and doggedness to allay misgivings on the latter score, though there was every reason to suppose that the Russians would prove doughty opponents. The quality of the British military command, however, was another matter altogether.

The Duke of Wellington had died in 1852, full of honours, the conqueror of Napoleon and the scourge of Chartists and Radicals. He was succeeded as Commander-in-Chief by Lord Raglan, whose chief merit lay in his long professional liaison with the Iron Duke. Raglan had served on the Duke's staff, and had subsequently filled the important administrative offices of Secretary-at-War and Master General of the Ordnance. He was sixty-six years of age when Britain entered the Crimean War, and had seen no active service since the Napoleonic Wars. On the field of Waterloo his right elbow had been shattered by a musket-ball, and he had let the surgeon amputate his damaged arm between the shoulder and the elbow without a murmur. As the surgeon tossed the arm away, Raglan called out, 'Hey, bring my arm back. There's a ring my wife gave me on the finger.'

So Raglan had an amazingly cool head and proven administrative ability, as well as the best possible social and military connexions. Yet for all this, and despite his evident care for the men under his command, Lord Raglan must bear considerable responsibility for the varied disasters of the Crimean campaign. His well-known tact and even temper, though suitable diplomatic weapons, were perhaps less effective instruments of command than outbreaks of fury or cold sarcasm. Raglan's defects would have mattered less if the commanders of the infantry and cavalry divisions had exhibited first-rate abilities.

Unfortunately, they did not. Only two of the five infantry divisional commanders had led anything larger than a battalion into action against properly trained opponents. Of these five officers, only one was under sixty years of age, and he had never seen action before; this was the Duke of Cambridge, aged thirty-four, Queen Victoria's cousin, the industrious and affable though inexperienced commander of the First Division. The sixty-six-year-old Sir George de Lacy Evans, commander of the Second Division, was intelligent, experienced, brusque and fairly radical – probably the ablest of them all. The Third Division was commanded by the mediocre Sir Richard England, who had been born in Canada sixty-one years before. The Hon. Sir George Cathcart, aged fifty-nine, led the Fourth Division, and was to prove irritable and obstinate under stress. The Fifth Division was commanded by the sixty-six-year-old Sir George Brown, as brave as a bull, but a renowned flogger, anti-reformer, martinet, and (in the words of one of his young officers) an 'old imbecile bully'.

Of the other commanding officers only the Hon. James Scarlett, aged fifty-five, who led the Heavy Cavalry Brigade, and the Chief Engineer, the seventy-two-year-old Sir John Burgoyne, inspired unqualified confidence; yet Scarlett had seen no active service, and Burgoyne was an old man. Lord Lucan, the commander of the Cavalry Division, was an obsessional officer of fifty-four years, with little military experience, though with enough cash to have once purchased the 17th Lancers for £25,000 and transformed them into gaudy dandies. His brother-in-law, Lord Cardigan, led the ill-fated Light Brigade; he was aged fifty-seven but had seen no active service; he was moreover an arrogant snob who excited even more hatred than Lucan.

There were other disadvantages for the British expeditionary force. The Commissariat Department of the army was quite inadequately staffed to cope with the demands of nearly thirty thousand troops campaigning at the edge of Asia – a fact with which Lord Raglan was well acquainted from his days as Master General of the Ordnance. Both the Ordnance and Commissariat

The Duke of Cambridge. The Queen's cousin and commander of the First Division.

departments were, in any case, responsible to Whitehall, as was the Army Medical Board. The Commander-in-Chief of the army was thus denied control over these essential supports for the fighting man, and was, in matters of supply, accountable to the Secretary-at-War who was in turn responsible to an overburdened Cabinet minister, the Secretary of State for War and the Colonies.

Inefficient as these administrative relationships were bound to be under serious stress, they were at least theoretically justifiable on the grounds that Parliament and the Civil Service should stand between the nation and military dictatorship. Inexcusable, save on the grounds of penny-pinching, was the decision taken after 1815 to scrap the Waggon Train and the Staff Corps. The Waggon Train had carried essential supplies to places of need during the Napoleonic Wars, and had also acted as an ambulance unit; the Staff Corps had provided some analysis of pressing military problems. The services of both were to be sorely needed in the Crimea.

To many French officers the British looked absurdly amateurish, and at least fifty years behind the times. Many officers brought their favourite horses, as if to hunt foxes; they also brought servants and tweed suits. Several brought their wives along too. The personal luggage of the British officers astounded the French, and it was noticed that the Duke of Cambridge's baggage filled seventeen carts.

Few of the British officers had any experience of active service against European opponents, and a good many had seen no active service at all – not even in India or the colonies. Far too many of the younger aristocratic officers had joined the army because it provided them with a suitable background for a fashionable and not too strenuous existence; certainly they set no great store on their professionalism. There were, of course, exceptions to this pattern, but there was a great deal of truth in the jibe that the wealthier officers treated their regiments as 'a lounge they had taken on lease'.

More than that, the system of buying commissions, which meant at the highest level the virtual purchase of regiments (£4,500 for the lieutenant-colonelcy of a regiment of the line, £6,175 for a cavalry regiment, and £9,000 for a regiment of Foot Guards), ensured the perpetuation of certain anomalies. For one thing, an able but impoverished ensign could find his way to promotion blocked by blue-blooded loafers who thought more of fox-hunting and gambling than of carrying out their regimental duties. For another, wealthy officers not only generally managed to avoid overseas service in unpopular stations like the West Indies, but also contrived lengthy periods of absence from duty when stationed in Britain. Regimental commanders, moreover, tended to view their units as their own property; they were frequently resentful of interference from above, and were often reluctant to join in large-scale practice

Roger Fenton, pioneer war photographer, aboard his photographic van.

manoeuvres which they considered to be 'a damned waste of time'. As for staff training, most officers considered it beneath them, or at best an irrelevancy; the Senior Department of the Royal Military College was sorely unattended, save for those who were obliged to take their careers in the army seriously.

Yet it was this army, indifferently and sometimes abominably led, over-disciplined, crammed with parade ground instruction, supported by a ludicrously inadequate administrative and supply organization, and in peace-time resented, if not openly despised, by the civilian population, that was now expected to achieve a quick and comprehensive victory over the Russians. In the circumstances, it is a remarkable tribute to the hardiness, resilience and loyalty of the British common soldier that he was able to more than hold his own in the Crimean campaign, and by his stoicism and strength under vile conditions cause a national outcry in favour of military reform.

The British army had one other ally apart from the French and the Turks in the Crimea. In May 1855 fifteen thousand Sardinian troops under General De La Marmora arrived at Balaclava. Count Cavour, Prime Minister of the united kingdom of Piedmont-Sardinia, was instrumental in dispatching these troops to the Crimea in order to achieve his country's representation at the eventual peace conference; by so doing Cavour, and his King, Victor Emmanuel II, hoped to advance Piedmont-Sardinia's claim to speak on behalf of the other states of a still disunited Italy.

Nor was this all. As sickness and battle casualties depleted the allied armies, there was a wholesale recruitment of mercenaries to fill the gaps. Thus side by side with the British, the French, the Turks and the Sardinians, fought fifteen hundred men of the Polish Legion, three thousand troops of the Swiss Legion, and about nine thousand men of the German Legion. It was, therefore, one of the smaller ironies of the campaign that Polish soldiers fought on both sides in a war to settle the fate of a failing Muslim power whose empire stretched from the Adriatic to the Persian Gulf.

As for the British redcoat, who was cheered to the echo as he marched off to embark for the eastern Mediterranean and death or glory, the whole business must have appeared singularly uninspiring, for although Russia was placed high in the national catalogue of demonology, the Turks were not unblemished allies. Perhaps Sergeant Timothy Gowing of the Royal Fusiliers spoke for many of his fellows when he wrote, 'We were going out to defend a rotten cause, a race that almost every Christian despises. However, as soldiers we had nothing to do with politics.'

Chapter 3

Landfall at Calamita Bay

Having declared war on Russia at the end of March 1854, the British government had no clear idea as to how or where to strike at the enemy, though in the same month Palmerston urged 'the advantage of a great attack on the Crimea'.

This was eventually the strategy decided upon; the vital Russian naval base in the Crimea, Sebastopol, would be taken, and the Russian government forced to agree to the allied peace terms. Palmerston was jauntily optimistic over the prospect, claiming that 'sixty thousand English and French troops, with the fleets co-operating, would accomplish the object in six weeks after landing, and if this blow was accompanied by successful operations in Georgia and Circassia, we might have a merry Christmas and a happy New Year'.

Between March 1854 and the eventual landing of the British and French forces at Calamita Bay on the Crimean peninsula in September, however, much occurred. On 31 March the first part of the British contingent sailed from Malta, arriving at the Dardanelles on 5 April and disembarking at Gallipoli. Here they found that French troops, having arrived first, had naturally taken the best billets. Both British and French were nonetheless desperately anxious to co-operate, and the first contacts between the allied troops were remarkably successful. Though the allied rank and file were hardly accomplished linguists, this proved no deterrent to friendship, and groups of French soldiers gabbled animatedly to equally vociferous British troops, neither understanding a word of what the other said.

There were, of course, notable differences between the allied forces, not least in the superior equipment and supplies of the French. The British at Gallipoli also tended to pay the asking price for local commodities, thus causing a ludicrous inflation in costs – a bottle of wine, for example, that had been priced at 4d. rocketed within a few days to nearly 2s. The French promptly insisted on fixing a tariff, which reduced the profits of the local traders – the Turks, widely considered by the allied troops to be 'a lazy, dirty, ungrateful lot', and the Greeks, 'much worse … and the greatest cheats going'.

Opposite Admiral Dundas, who first served with the Black Sea Fleet, and then commanded the Baltic Fleet.

One other early contrast between the allies was in the deportment of their senior officers. When Prince Napoleon, the commander of the French 3rd Division, landed at Gallipoli, he clattered royally ashore, all gold lace and plumes, and was greeted by an Imperial salute from the guns of five French men-of-war. Lord Raglan's arrival was much more discreet, almost furtive; he stepped ashore in his plain blue frock coat to be welcomed merely by Mrs Estcourt, his Adjutant-General's wife; he then walked up to the town with Mrs Estcourt and his four young aides-de-camp (his nephews). When, a week later, the Duke of Cambridge (Queen Victoria's cousin) arrived, he also landed modestly, striking an onlooker as 'a quiet looking gentleman in a tweed jacket'.

As more British forces arrived, they were moved on to Constantinople, and eventually to nearby Scutari on the other side of the Bosphorus. To the officers and men a new and amazing world was opened up to them. Though Constantinople seemed, from the sea, a city of delicate minarets, cypress groves and exotic vegetation, its blue skies swept with plovers and storks, the reality was different. Soldiers soon discovered that the streets were filthy, and often so badly paved as to be downright dangerous. Men stumbled to avoid dead rats and dogs, and the pushing, jostling crowds, but there was no avoiding the stench that assailed their nostrils.

Of course, there were compensations. In the narrow, dirty back streets the troops were able to find cheap wine and cheap whores, and it was soon reckoned that you could get drunk for sixpence and syphilis for a shilling. Drunkenness was to be expected, though the intoxicated soldiery tended to knock the Turks about and a few offenders had to be flogged as a warning. Syphilis was more of a problem, but unavoidable in a society where sumptuous and (doubtless) uncontaminated women were veiled and bundled up in flowing robes, showing at best their ankles – which one British officer described (possibly from pique) as 'for the most part decidedly bad, thick and clumsy; feet ditto'.

Scutari, where the British forces were soon to be concentrated, was no paradise either. Lord Raglan described his headquarters as a 'furiously hot' wooden building, 'low on the beach where all the filth of Constantinople is driven either by the wind or the current and so great is the abominable smell thereof that for the last ten days I have been driven from the room I used to sit in and have been forced to receive and transact business in my bedroom'. The British troops at Scutari were encamped either behind Lord Raglan's house, or in and around the great Turkish army barracks which were soon to become the notorious hospital for the reception of the British sick and wounded. Among the British forces passed Jewish money-changers, and assorted Turks, Greeks and Armenians peddling wares ranging from sherbet to horses, and from lemonade to young girls.

In the middle of May, as the weather grew hotter and more oppressive, Lord Raglan conferred with his allied counterparts,

Marshal St Arnaud and the Turkish commander Omar Pasha (born Michael Lattas, the Greek Orthodox son of a Croatian soldier in the Austrian army). The three men agreed that the Anglo-French army should sail to the Black Sea port of Varna, in what is now modern Bulgaria; from there the allies could advance to relieve the Russian siege of the strategically important fortified town of Silistria situated on the Danube.

Despite this early agreement, Lord Raglan encountered some immediate difficulties with the French high command. St Arnaud and his senior ADC Colonel Trochu, the Emperor's confidant, attempted to persuade Raglan to alter the arrangement for a joint descent on Varna. Instead the French high command wished to send only one division to Varna, and to move the rest of the French army to a defensive position behind the Balkan range and based on Bourgas; indeed one division, under General Bosquet, had already set off for Adrianople and was beyond recall. Raglan politely, steadily and persuasively opposed these French moves.

Cookhouse of the 8th Hussars.

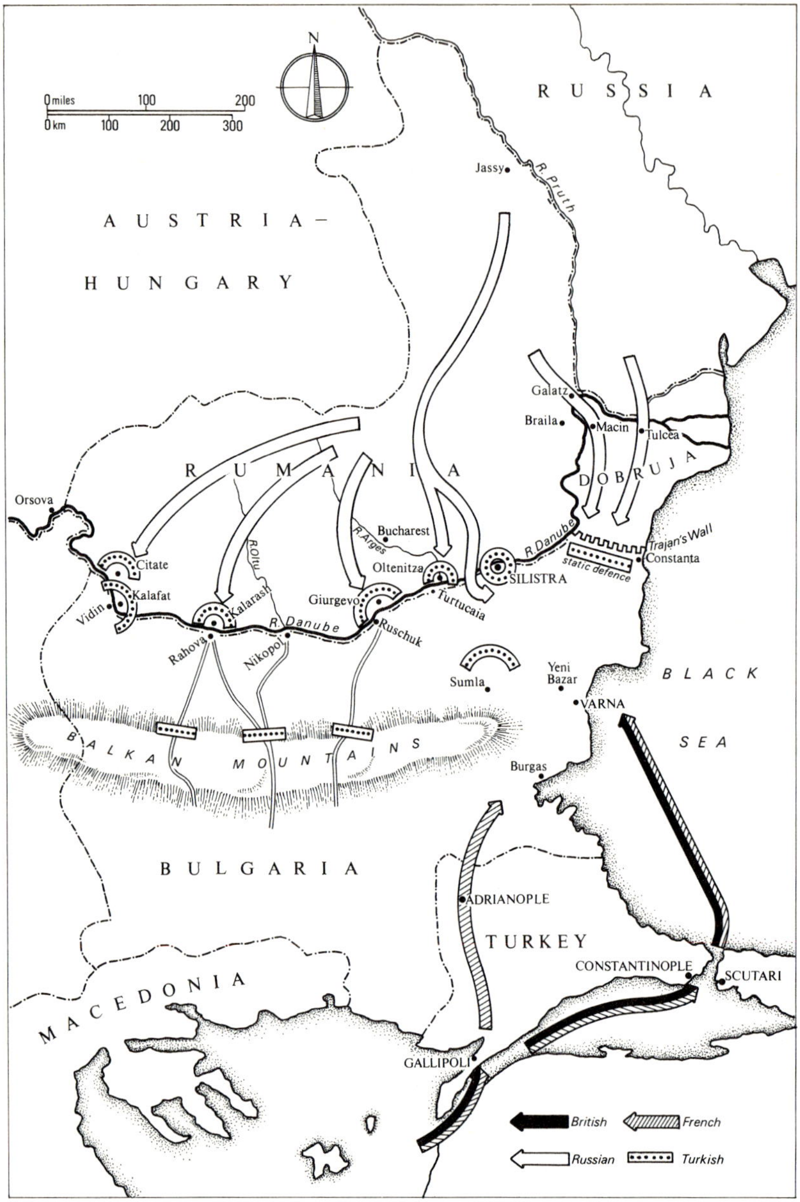

The Danube theatre of the war.

Eventually he won his case, just as he had earlier rebuffed St Arnaud's suggestion that when the British and French troops went into action together the French commander should be the superior. One of the chief reasons why Lord Raglan was able to assert his point of view with such success on these and other occasions lay in his capacity to make those who disagreed with him at the same time anxious not to displease him. He was thus able to exert considerable influence over men as diverse as St Arnaud and Omar Pasha; though on some occasions they were puzzled as to his real feelings.

At any rate, on 28 May the British and French forces were committed to the move to Varna. Their landing on the Bulgarian coast coincided with, and lent great moral support to, a determined Turkish attempt to raise the siege of Silistria. A small Turkish force managed to enter the beleaguered town, and give fresh heart to its exhausted defenders. On 22 June, the Russian commander Prince Gorchakov ordered a final desperate assault; the attack failed, Gorchakov was wounded and the next day the Russian forces began retreating to the north. Silistria was saved. So, ten days later, were the Danubian provinces, for the Turks proceeded to defeat their enemies in the field; by 11 July the Russians were in full retreat towards Bucharest; they then abandoned Moldavia and Wallachia. The main object of the Anglo-French intervention in the war now seemed fulfilled: the Turkish Empire was saved, and the Russians driven back across the Pruth.

It would have been happier for all concerned if the war had gone no further. But the allied governments were now convinced that Sebastopol must be taken and the Russian fleet destroyed; though the British Prime Minister Lord Aberdeen remained reluctant to see a substantial extension of the war, his views were unpopular, and *Punch* showed him blacking the Tsar's boots. In Britain crowds demonstrated in favour of continuing the war, and Queen Victoria told her uncle Leopold, King of the Belgians, that the war 'was popular beyond belief'. In anticipation of protracted hostilities the Chancellor of the Exchequer, William Ewart Gladstone, had raised the rate of income tax from 7d. to 1s. 2d. in the pound.

On 28 June the Cabinet authorised Lord Raglan to invade the Crimea. They did so in circumstances far removed from war fever, for as the Duke of Newcastle, Secretary of State for War, read out the draft dispatch he intended sending to Lord Raglan most of his Cabinet colleagues unashamedly dozed in their chairs, though they later stirred themselves and declared that they were well satisfied with the document. From France, Napoleon III, anxious for his armies to get into spectacular action, similarly instructed St Arnaud to prepare to embark at Varna, though the rest of the telegram was indecipherable and it was left to Lord Raglan to confirm the decision to invade the Crimea.

Two months elapsed between the decision to strike at Sebastopol and the embarkation of the allied armies at Varna. For the allied soldiers, Varna had first seemed like a demi-paradise after Scutari. The little town was beautiful, and the surrounding fertile countryside produced a profusion of crops including corn, grapes, melons, cucumbers, Indian corn, barley and oats. The Bulgarians, in their sheepskin caps, seemed friendly and patient, and were paid handsomely for the local transport facilities they provided for the allied armies. The troops bathed in the warm sea, fished in the lakes for carp and bream, and hunted wild boar in the woods.

Relations between the British, French and Turkish troops continued to be extremely cordial. Marshal St Arnaud was greeted by thunderous cheers whenever he rode through the British lines, and shouted in reply 'England for ever!' The Turkish Commander-in-Chief, Omar Pasha, was equally popular, and was described by a young British officer as 'a capital fellow. Quite different from the Turks in general... He is a sporting looking fellow and sits well on his horse in a plain grey frock-coat and long jack boots, he is very fond of horses.' Omar Pasha was equally complimentary towards the British troops, declaring that 'the Emperor of Russia is mad, but surely he cannot be mad enough to fight against troops like these'. For his part, Lord Raglan was less sure about the qualities of the Turkish troops; in particular, he disliked the brutality with which the Bashi-Bazouks treated the Bulgarians, and resisted suggestions that some units of these ferocious irregulars should be attached to the British army.

As July wore on the mood of the encamped armies changed. The heat enervated the troops, and they were pestered by flies, gnats and leeches. Though officers were forbidden to wear civilian clothes, many of them wound protective turbans round their forage caps and refused to button up their tunics. Beards and whiskers sprouted in profusion despite the vehement disapproval of the rigid commander of the 5th (Light) Division, Sir George Brown. The men were bored and weary, and a major of the 8th Hussars wrote home languidly, 'No doubt we shall go soon, but such is the state of apathy that we are reduced to, that no one seems to care whether we go to Sebastopol or South America or stay as we are or do nothing.'

The Times' correspondent, the redoubtable and sharp-sighted William Howard Russell, had already observed the shortcomings in British organisation at Varna:

> Where is the English post office? No one knows. Where does the English General live? No one knows. Where is the hospital to carry a sick soldier to? No one knows. Where are the field hospitals? At present if a serious case of illness occurs in camp, the only conveyance for the sufferer is a

Lord Aberdeen, Prime Minister until February 1855, by J. Partridge.

bullock cart, and in that miserable springless vehicle he has to perform the tedious journey into Varna – enough to destroy all chance of recovery.

For some time many of the men had suffered from diarrhoea and nausea which left them exhausted and listless. Then, on 19 July, there was a serious outbreak of cholera in the French camp. Cholera outbreaks had occurred throughout southern Europe that summer, and the disease had a fearsome reputation; carried in water, the infection could strike with unpredictable savagery and turn a healthy man into a blackened, dehydrated corpse, ready for burning, within a few hours. On 22 July cholera struck the British encampments, and though the tents were moved, the disease could not be shaken off.

By the beginning of August the situation had deteriorated sharply and William Russell wrote:

The cholera continues. The 50th Regiment ... lost nine men last night

> … it is useless to alarm friends and relations at home by talking of the number of sick or giving their names, but it is evident that we are in a very unsatisfactory state as regards health … At present the cholera has assumed a phase which baffles our best efforts, and throws all our past data to the winds. It is sometimes quite painless, there is little or no purging but the sufferer is seized with violent spasms in the stomach, which increase in intensity till collapse is established, and death then rapidly follows, attended with but little exhibitions of agony.

As the temperature soared to 90° Fahrenheit, the army battled against lethargy, boredom and disease. Men struggled through their duties, with pale, gaunt faces; sometimes they were too exhausted to eat the extra meat rations that had been provided to boost their morale, and myriads of insects settled on the discarded lumps of food.

Still the cholera raged. The commander of one of the British line regiments noted crisply: 'Cholera increasing, and men dying fast. Every case taken in at the General Hospital in Varna has gone to the grave. Fifteen dead last two nights.' The hospital at Varna was a converted barracks that soon acquired a dreadful reputation as a veritable morgue: the orderlies were often too listless to attend to their stricken patients, who tossed and turned on their sweat-soaked mattresses; the rotten floorboards harboured lice, fleas and huge grey rats.

These were conditions that presaged the horrors of the hospital at Scutari later in the campaign, but surprisingly little seems to have been learnt from the grisly lesson at Varna. The British soldiers soon became convinced that once they were carried through the doors of the hospital they would never come out alive. They consequently strove to disguise the onset of illness, thus increasing the chances of infecting their fellows. As a desperate preventative, the troops drank the coarse local brandy, which could be purchased at 3s. 6d. a bottle, and which was considered safer than the red wine drunk by the French. But the brandy did not stay the cholera, and instead the camp sites became littered with drunken men sleeping under the scorching sun while hosts of insects crawled over them.

To add to the discomforts of the army, on 10 August a fire broke out at Varna consuming a considerable amount of stores, including sixteen thousand pairs of boots and 150 tons of biscuits. It was reckoned that local Greeks, who hated their Turkish overlords and their new allies, had started the fire; indeed, five of them had been caught red-handed by the French and bayoneted on the spot, causing the cavalryman Lord George Paget to remark, somewhat enviously, 'They do things better than we do in this army.'

The redoubtable *Times* correspondent, W. H. Russell.

One way of lifting the troops' spirits, and shaking off disease, was to leave Varna for the Crimea. The British and French governments had already instructed their commanders to prepare for this move, and the Duke of Newcastle's letter to Lord Raglan had urged an early assault on Sebastopol:

> I have on the part of Her Majesty's Government [the Duke had written] to instruct your lordship to concert measures for the siege of Sebastopol, unless, with the information in your possession but at present unknown in this country, you should be decidedly of opinion that it could not be undertaken with a reasonable prospect of success.

> The confidence with which Her Majesty placed under your command the gallant army now in Turkey is unabated; and if, upon mature reflection, you should consider that the united strength of the two armies is insufficient for this undertaking, you are not to be precluded from the exercise of the discretion originally vested in you, though Her Majesty's Government will learn with regret that an attack, from which such important consequences are anticipated, must be any longer delayed.
>
> The difficulties of the siege of Sebastopol appear to Her Majesty's Government to be more likely to increase than to diminish by delay; and as there is no prospect of a safe and honourable peace until the fortress is reduced and the fleet taken or destroyed, it is, on all accounts, most important that nothing but insuperable impediments – such as the want of ample preparations by either army, or the possession by Russia of a force in the Crimea greatly out-numbering that which can be brought against it – should be allowed to prevent the early decision to undertake these operations.

Lord Raglan had little alternative but to accept these urgings, though he had grave misgivings over the projected invasion. For one thing, the allies were ignorant as to the strength of the Russian forces that would oppose them. St Arnaud had heard the rumour that there were seventy thousand Russian troops in the Crimea; the commander of the British support fleet, Vice-Admiral Dundas, believed that there were over 140,000; the Duke of Newcastle considered the Foreign Office estimate of forty-five thousand to be the most likely.

Summoning Sir George Brown to confer with him, Lord Raglan confessed his disquiet, and asked his forthright colleague how their late mentor, the Duke of Wellington, would have acted. Sir George replied that he believed the Iron Duke would not have budged without more information, but added that in this case the Cabinet could probably replace Lord Raglan with a more compliant Commander-in-Chief if he failed to carry out its wishes. Raglan appreciated the force of this argument. But there were other reasons for quitting Varna which seemed to him conclusive, notably that the troops' discipline was suffering from their enforced inactivity just as much as their health.

Lord Raglan, together with Marshal St Arnaud, therefore came to the decision to press ahead with the invasion of the Crimea, though (as he told the Duke of Newcastle) 'more in deference to the views of the British Government' and to the 'acquiescence of the Emperor Louis Napoleon in those views' than in response to his own better judgement.

The allies began to plan the departure of their forces. The original sailing date was fixed for 2 September 1854, and on 24 August the troops began the lengthy process of embarkation. The British had twenty-seven thousand men fit for action, the French thirty thousand, and the Turks contributed seven thousand. By no means all the men who had originally landed at Varna now left it. Apart from those who had died of cholera in the encampments, the French had launched an ill-judged and vainglorious invasion of the flat Dobrudja region in what is today Romania. The French commanders had argued that the foray would divert attention from the allies' preparations to invade the Crimea, but the British high command suspected Marshal St Arnaud of making a premature bid for military glory. At any rate, the three French divisions achieved very little; they sighted a few Cossack patrols, but the main body of the Russian forces was well across the Danube; as the French turned back towards Varna cholera dogged them, turning the retreat into a funeral march, with thousands perishing on the way – it is estimated that the 1st French Division lost six thousand men.

The Russians were not deceived by this feint into the Dobrudja; their enemies were expected to attack the base at Sebastopol, and this prediction was conveniently confirmed by *The Times* announcing the fact beforehand, thus moving the Duke of Newcastle to tell Lord Raglan 'I am grieved beyond measure at the unpatriotic conduct of *The Times*... proclaiming to the Emperor the attack on the Crimea... I believe it is a mere guess on its part but every sovereign nation thinks *The Times* is in the confidence of the Government.' Although the allied troops did not formally know until 25 August that Sebastopol was definitely their objective, and some believed they were to be sent to Odessa, it came as no surprise that the scaling ladders and gabions (earth-filled wicker baskets to afford protection against rifle fire) that they had been ordered to make were to be used against Russia's great naval base in the Crimea.

The British troops were overjoyed at the prospect of leaving Varna behind them. 'Hurrah for the Crimea!' wrote Cornet Fisher. 'We are off tomorrow. Take Sebastopol in a week or so, and then into winter quarters.' As the men boarded the vessels which were to take them to the Crimea, they saw on all sides such an impressive assembly of transport ships and men-of-war, with hundreds of small boats bobbing between them, that an army surgeon wrote to his sister that 'Such a sight was never seen since before the foundation of the world – magnificent – impossible to describe... How they can resist such a force as ours I know not. Failure seems impossible.'

Major-General Estcourt, Raglan's much criticised Adjutant-General.

Although the force was embarked by 5 September it was not until dawn on 7 September that Admiral Dundas gave the signal to weigh anchor, and, with bands playing, the steamers began to tow the sailing ships out to sea. St Arnaud, already failing in strength, had impatiently set out on 5 September in the *Ville de Paris*, but on 8 September there was a rendezvous with Lord Raglan who was aboard the *Caradoc*. However, St Arnaud was too ill to board the *Caradoc*, and Lord Raglan, with only one arm, could not clamber up the side of the French three-decker tossing in a rough sea. This was inconvenient, to say the least, for amazingly the allied armies had set sail from Varna with their landing place on the Crimean peninsula still to be decided upon!

The problem was resolved by the passing of messages between the two ships, and finally the French second-in-command, General Canrobert, came aboard the *Caradoc*, which then steamed off on

8 September on a reconnaissance. Prudently flying the Russian flag, the *Caradoc* chugged past Sebastopol, which seemed to be bristling with guns, and stopped just north of the city to survey a possible landing place at the mouth of the Katcha river. The spot was considered unsuitable, however, and the *Caradoc* moved off to the north, its progress followed by astounded Russian spectators who had never seen an iron ship of this type before. Some thirty-five miles to the north of Sebastopol, south of Eupatoria, the ship reached a long sandy beach where naked men and women were bathing together. Lord Raglan promptly made the decision which shattered the idyllic calm of Calamita Bay; he announced that the allied armies would be put ashore here at the Old Fort within the next few days, where the salt lake of Kamishla would protect the expedition's left flank.

On 12 September the allied armada closed in on the small undefended port of Eupatoria, where the mayor was handed a summons to surrender. This worthy official first insisted on fumigating the summons in accordance with local health regulations; he then read the document, and told the Anglo-French delegation that they could land, but must consider themselves in quarantine.

The disembarkation began at dawn on 14 September. It was unopposed, and almost ignored, save for a group of Cossacks who watched the start of the proceeding from their shaggy ponies while their elegant officer jotted down some notes. Apart from this, the countryside beyond the beaches looked peaceful and sparsely tenanted, with flocks of sheep and herds of cattle grazing amid the pastures. The French were the first to land, and at 8.30 am they planted the tricolour on the beach; within an hour nine thousand French troops were ashore, and their advanced positions were three or four miles inland.

The British landing went less smoothly. It had been arranged that a buoy should be placed opposite the Old Fort, and that the French would disembark to the right of the buoy and the British to the left. During the night, however, the buoy had mysteriously moved to the north, and the British (who were suspicious that the French had done this) were eventually forced to land on a beach separated from their allies by a low bluff. After this unexpected hitch, though, the landing went well enough. On a mile-wide front, scores of rowing boats ferried the men ashore; the troops were lifted onto the beach by sailors who, perhaps conscious of the fact that they were not likely to get involved in the land fighting, were particularly jovial, calling out 'Come on, girls!' to the kilted Highlanders.

But as the British troops moved away from their landing places some of their high spirits evaporated. For one thing, each man was in full dress and staggering under a daunting weight of equipment that comprised four-and-a-half pounds of salt beef and the same weight of biscuit; his greatcoat and blanket rolled up in a knapsack which also contained a spare pair of boots, spare socks, shirt and forage cap; a water canteen; part of his mess's cooking apparatus; a rifle and bayonet, and fifty rounds of ammunition for the Minié or sixty rounds for the smoothbore musket which some units still carried.

By noon the sun disappeared behind dark clouds and a fine rain began to fall. Already some sick men had collapsed and were being taken back to the boats. As night fell, the rain began to pour down on the huddled army, many of whom were trying to light fires with damp wood. As the British troops sought for shelter or resignedly lay down to sleep under the downpour, their French comrades were able to crawl under their 'dog tents' which each of them carried.

The rain fortunately stopped at dawn on 15 September. During that day the British, who had already landed their infantry and some of their artillery, now began to get the cavalry ashore. This was no mean feat since the horses were terrified of the rough sea and proved very difficult to handle; several boats carrying horses were overturned and it was decided to land the remaining animals when the sea grew calmer. By nightfall on the following day, however, the rest of the cavalry had landed, and most of the army's stores were ashore.

Landing allied troops at Calamita Bay, September 1854.

Though the French were anxious to move off south towards Sebastopol, the British were not ready to strike out until 19 September. Much of the time between 15 and 19 September had been spent by the British forces in rounding up more wagons, carts, baggage animals, drivers and a variety of supplies. The newly appointed Quartermaster-General, the energetic and apparently able General Airey, at fifty-one years old one of the youngest of the British expedition's senior officers, did his best to scour the surrounding countryside for the necessary supplies. But even though

Major-General Airey, the controversial Quartermaster-General.

the twenty-seven thousand British troops could eventually count on 350 wagons, 67 camels, 253 horses, 45 cartloads of poultry, corn and flour, and a thousand head of cattle and sheep, it was evident that this would be barely adequate. One reason for this shortage was that the French were ruthless in their commandeering of local supplies; sometimes they paid their own price, sometimes they paid nothing at all. Lord Raglan disapproved strongly of the plundering habits of the French, and tried to restrain his own men from similar activities.

At last, on 19 September, the British forces were ready to move. Reveille was sounded at 3 am, but the advance did not begin until 9 o'clock. During these six hours, the French, who had chafed for the last two days at the British army's inability to advance, were again ready well before their allies, and beat their drums impatiently while the British extricated themselves from their now traditional confusion.

The sun blazed down when at last the preoccupied and uncharacteristically curt Lord Raglan rode off in front of his columns, with the French and Turkish forces on his right nearest the sea. As they set off, an onlooker wrote an almost lyrical description:

> The September sun shone brightly on a forest of bayonets: and while the eye rested with delight on grand and imposing masses of colour, blended yet contrasted, the ear drank in a volume of sound in which the shrill notes of innumerable bugles, and the roll of countless drums, were now lost, now harmonized, in the multitudinous hum of the armed force on the march.

But the men were soon parched and weary, and now and then one of them would stumble out of the ranks and collapse, attacked by cholera. In the early afternoon, the allies made their first contact with the Russians on the river Bulganek. The British cavalry, their coordination already marred by the sharp hostility that existed between the brothers-in-law Lords Lucan and Cardigan, were anxious to charge a force of two thousand Russian cavalry that appeared below them on the south bank of the Bulganek. But Lord Raglan, on higher ground, spotted six thousand men of the Russian 17th Division beyond their cavalry, and ordered Lord Lucan and Lord Cardigan to withdraw. A fitful artillery duel followed, which the British won. The Russians then withdrew to their main position across the river Alma, where they hoped to thwart the allied advance on Sebastopol. The allied armies settled down for a night's rest, from which the British emerged next morning chilled and without a properly prepared breakfast, while the French had been kept warm and dry, and were more than adequately fed. At any rate, both armies, and their accompanying Turkish units, now prepared, on 20 September, to march against the enemy upon the southern bank of the river Alma.

Chapter 4

On the Banks of the Alma

At seven o'clock on the morning of 20 September the British forces on the north bank of the Alma were roused from their uncomfortable sleep. Not all of them, however, had survived the night, and by eight o'clock three hundred or so cholera victims, dead or dying, lay separated from their fellows. By nine o'clock the British regiments that had bivouacked to the east to protect the army's flank began marching into line with the rest of the forces. The French, of course, were up and ready long before these manoeuvres began, and General Bosquet's division, which had been in battle order since dawn, settled down to make its morning coffee as a diversion. Finally, at 11.30 am, the British forces had drawn level with their French and Turkish allies, and the advance towards the Alma began.

The ground between the British army and the north bank of the river sloped gently down, the green countryside dotted with vineyards and small whitewashed houses. The Russian position across the river, however, was in stark contrast; here the land rose sharply to a high plateau, and the steep, rocky slopes promised a hard climb. This formidable escarpment ran for four thousand yards from the sea, pierced at a few points by roads or tracks of which the most important was the Causeway, the main post road from Eupatoria to Sebastopol. To the right of the Causeway a track wound up the slope towards the heights where the Russians had constructed a telegraph station – which became known as the Telegraph Height. To the left of the Causeway the ground, though steep, was no longer precipitous, and was dominated by a great shoulder of hillside, known as Kourgané Hill, which thrust obliquely towards the village of Bourliuk; on the lower slopes of this rocky shoulder, the Russians had thrown up two earthworks known as the Great and Lesser Redoubts. Both the Russian commander, Prince Menshikov, and Lord Raglan saw Kourgané Hill as the key position in the approaching engagement. Against the sea stood the towering granite face of the West Cliff which Menshikov considered inaccessible to infantry and artillery, and therefore left undefended, save for a small detachment in the village of Ulukul Akles.

Opposite The heights of the Alma, by Orlando Norrie.

The Russian commander, in fact, placed only one battalion of the Minsk Regiment between the Causeway and the West Cliff. Instead he concentrated his forces astride the Causeway, making his headquarters on Kourgané Hill; to the left were the troops of the Russian centre commanded by General Kvetinski, while to their left forces led by General Kirakov guarded the Telegraph

Prince Menshikov, Russian commander in the Crimea at the outset of the war.

Height. Menshikov's position gave him considerable satisfaction. He believed that the allied forces would be repelled with terrible losses when they assaulted the stony ridges across the Alma (which was shallow and easily forded). It was a prospect which afforded him a grim satisfaction, since his arrogant and bullying manner owed something at least to his earlier castration by a Turkish roundshot, and he had come to hate the Turks and any allies of theirs with a consuming passion – perhaps one of the few he had left.

The allied commanders had conferred late on the previous night, and had evolved a plan of action which, unfortunately, had been left somewhat blurred. Marshal St Arnaud had proposed the tactics for the imminent battle in a flood of excited rhetoric. The French plan was perfectly straightforward: their forces would attack on the right, next to the sea and protected by the guns of the fleet; they would strike through the village of Almatamak, scale the West Cliff and roll up the Russian left flank; meanwhile, the British would advance against the Russian centre and right flank; the Russians would thus be caught, and crushed, in a pincer movement.

Lord Raglan had listened to these impassioned arguments (which one of his officers thought were partly affected by drugs) with his customary politeness. Privately he considered that St Arnaud had gravely underestimated the strength of the Russian positions in front of the British troops. But, not wishing to precipitate an unseemly altercation, he contented himself with assuring the French that they could rely on the 'vigorous cooperation' of the British army. St Arnaud therefore left the British lines not really knowing whether or not his plan had been fully understood or accepted.

Next morning, as the allied armies began to advance in silence, without drum or bugle, on a front nearly five miles across, St Arnaud was still unsure as to Lord Raglan's precise intentions. Nonetheless, he was confident of a great victory, and took fresh heart from the lusty cheers of those British regiments whose path he rode across, shouting back, with hardly an accent, 'Hurrah for old England!'

Soon after midday, as the allied fleet opened fire on the seaward flank, Lord Raglan and St Arnaud met to clarify the position. The British advance was halted while the two commanders conferred, St Arnaud talking animatedly to the staid, frock-coated Raglan. St Arnaud was trying to discover whether the British would turn the Russian right flank or attack the centre; Raglan replied somewhat evasively that he thought the flanking movement too difficult, and that he would prefer to see how the battle developed before committing himself further. St Arnaud was still not absolutely sure, therefore, of Raglan's precise intentions – but, then, neither was Raglan himself.

At 1 pm the advance began again, but soon the leading detachments of the Rifle Brigade came under rifle fire from Russians on the river banks. The British army halted, and deployed from column into line to make a less concentrated target for the enemy's marksmen as well as for the Russian artillery which was trying to find the range.

On the British right, however, the French kept their densely packed column formation, followed by the Turkish battalions. General Bosquet's 2nd Division was nearest the sea, while on his left General Canrobert's 1st Division and Prince Napoleon's 3rd Division approached the Alma past the White Farm; General Forey's 4th Division was in reserve. Of these forces only the 3rd Division was coming under fire.

The Russians were impressed by the approaching French forces. The British advance, however, was a less awesome spectacle. For

one thing, the British divisions were strung out in straggling red lines: de Lacy Evans' 2nd Division was nearing the village of Bourliuk on a front one thousand yards across; on their left, Sir George Brown's Light Division was spread out, two deep, along a mile-long front; behind these two divisions the 1st Division, led by the Duke of Cambridge, was deployed on a front of three thousand yards; the 3rd Division, under Sir Richard England, was in reserve on the Causeway road, and Sir George Cathcart's 4th Division was drawn up in column on the left flank, to the left of the leading divisions, and covered by the Cavalry Division under Lord Lucan; each division was accompanied by its own artillery.

The allied attack at the Alma.

What the Russians could not see was that the extreme right flank lines of the Light Division were becoming inextricably entangled with the left flank lines of the 2nd Division. Sir George Brown, the irascible commander of the Light Division, was not only notoriously short-sighted, but also refused to wear spectacles; he was, moreover, extremely touchy when offered advice. Lord Raglan, who perceived that the Light and the Second Divisions were now jostling each others' elbows, tried to rectify matters by riding to find Brown himself. Unfortunately he was only able to make contact with General Codrington, the commander of the Light Division's 1st Brigade, and, fearing to provoke Brown with an order delivered by a subordinate officer, he finally failed to sort out the confusion, and the two divisions lurched towards the river as entangled as before. Behind these advancing units, the Duke of Cambridge had ordered the 1st Division to spread out so far to right and left that on its right flank it obstructed some of the ground into which the 3rd Division was expected to march.

At any rate, the advancing British troops had speedily taken on the appearance of a blundering rabble. More than that, they were now, amazingly so the Russians thought, lying down under artillery fire. Lord Raglan had decided that his troops should wait for the French advance on the right flank to have its effect before committing the British army to a full frontal attack. For an hour and a half, the troops lay patiently under fire, doing their best to avoid the roundshot that bounced and whistled about their ears, and calling out to their mounted officers behind them warnings as to the direction of particular shots.

Battle of the Alma, the troops being supported by allied warships.

If many of the British troops were undergoing a baptism of fire, Lord Raglan himself was about to go into action for the first time

for nearly forty years. He was, despite this, remarkably cool and fearless; he moved round freely, accompanied by his staff officers, and apparently unruffled by the fire directed at his head. Lord Raglan's composed and polite bearing was about to be tested, for, far to his right, the French stood poised between remarkable success and dire confusion. On the extreme right flank of the allied advance, Bosquet's division had scaled the West Cliff and had dragged twelve guns with them. Prince Menshikov was staggered at the news of Bosquet's success, and at first refused to believe it. He galloped off, however, to see for himself, ordering eight reserve battalions to accompany him. On discovering that Bosquet had indeed turned his left flank, the nearly hysterical Russian Commander-in-Chief turned back leaving the French in possession of the ground they had won.

But although Bosquet had achieved a striking success on the right flank, he needed reinforcements in order to push on and roll up the Russian left. Reinforcements, however, were slow to arrive. Marshal St Arnaud had indeed urged General Canrobert's 1st

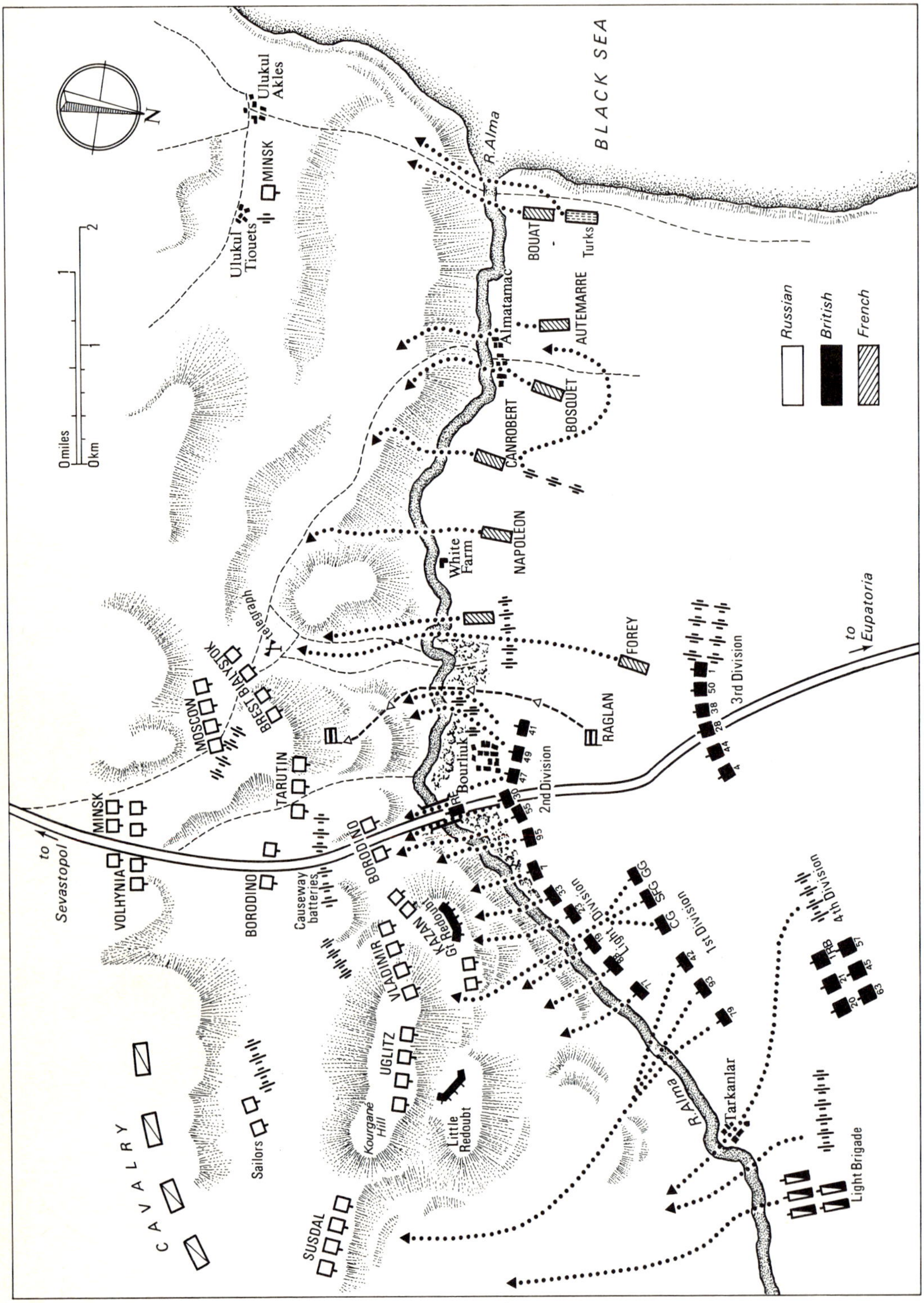

The Battle of the Alma.

Division and Prince Napoleon's 3rd Division across the Alma with the flattering but imprecise words, 'With men such as you I have no orders to give. I have but to point at the enemy.' But soon both divisions were in trouble: Canrobert struggled up towards the Telegraph Height, without his guns, which were diverted to an easier route; Napoleon's troops came under such heavy fire from Telegraph Height that they made little progress and hung back considerably discouraged. To add to the confusion, St Arnaud sent off General Forey's reserve 4th Division in support of Bosquet and Canrobert and these troops began to crowd into an already congested front to the right of the blazing and abandoned village of Burliuk.

If Prince Menshikov had been calmly surveying the situation, instead of galloping frantically across his front, he might well have won the day. For with the French and British in considerable difficulties on either side of the Causeway, the Russians could probably have driven Bosquet off the West Cliff and hurled their cavalry against the British left flank to great effect.

In fact, Lord Raglan had by now grown tired of waiting; he had, moreover, just received a French aide-de-camp who had informed him that Bosquet's men would have to retreat unless they were given prompt support. So Raglan sent General Airey's aide-de-camp, the impetuous and ill-fated Captain Nolan, to order the British regiments to advance once more. Across a two-mile front the British lines rose, dressed rank, and, two-deep, marched down to the river Alma.

The sun was now burning down on the thirsty troops as they approached the river; some cast aside knapsacks and shakos, and a few fainted and collapsed. In front of the Light Division and the 2nd Division there was the village of Bourliuk, still burning fiercely, and nearby, orchards and vineyards, which were difficult to pass through in good order. De Lacy Evans' 2nd Division struggled round both sides of Bourliuk, where they came under fire from the Russian guns across the river; the 2nd Brigade suffered heavily, losing a quarter of its men.

To the left of the 2nd Division, Sir George Brown's Light Division were (appropriately enough) making quicker progress. Though the river bed at this point was of variable depth, and some men lost their footing and were swept off and drowned, the Light Division splashed its way across the Alma, the troops holding their rifles and ammunition above their heads. Once across the river, however, the men found themselves crushed together in confusion under the high bank on the opposite side. Here General Codrington,

Fording the Alma, by
Louis A. Johns.

the tight-lipped commander of the division's 1st Brigade, took matters into his own hands and yelled at his men, and any others that had become mixed up with them, 'Fix bayonets! Get up the bank and advance to the attack.'

As the troops advanced towards the Great Redoubt they saw on either side two densely packed columns of the Kazan Regiment, their long yellowish-grey overcoats reaching to their ankles. On the Great Redoubt itself the Russian guns were waiting for their skirmishers to withdraw up the slope to safety before opening fire. Seeing this, the British officers and NCOs began to spread their men out into extended, and hence less vulnerable, lines.

But before the Russian guns opened fire the right hand column of the Kazan Regiment started to move down the slope, like some ponderous juggernaut, towards the advancing red lines. The British troops were undismayed and began shooting calmly and accurately into the Russian ranks. Surprisingly the Russians stopped, and then lumbered back into their original position.

The 1st Brigade surged forward, until they were so close that the men could see that the white faces of the Russian troops opposite them were topped by spiked helmets with small brass badges. Then the Russian guns opened fire, and roundshot began to crash into the British lines as they came on as before. Gaps appeared in the lines as men were brought down. In front of them rode Sir George Brown, red-faced and furious, on his grey horse; beside him rode General Codrington on his white Arab, while further to the left Colonel Lacy Yea of the 7th Fusiliers vociferously urged his men on, and, though hit on the belt buckle by a musket-ball, shouted at a wounded fellow-officer, 'Damn you! Damn you! Why don't you come? I've got a bullet in my guts but I'm going on.'

As the 7th Fusiliers began to exchange rifle shots with the troops of the Kazan Regiment, other units of the Light Division heard the unmistakable sounds of the Russian guns being pulled out of the Great Redoubt. With renewed energy they hurled themselves at the earthen parapets of the Redoubt, and captured it. The overjoyed men cheered and shouted, and some scratched their names on the brass barrel of an abandoned Russian howitzer. Their rejoicing, however, was likely to be short-lived unless they were promptly reinforced.

Unfortunately there was no sign of immediate support. The 1st Division, led by the royal Duke of Cambridge, had not supported 'the Light Division in its forward movement' as ordered. Indeed their advance had ground to a halt before they had reached the Alma. There were several reasons for this: the Duke of Cambridge was inexperienced, and, lacking clear instructions, fearful of making an unforgivable blunder; also the Guards Brigade, on the right of the 1st Division's line, had originally come under heavy artillery fire from the Great Redoubt and the Causeway. General Buller, of the Light Division, who had also failed to back up the advance of his division's 1st Brigade, hung back too, though advising the anxious Duke of Cambridge to move forward.

General Airey now rode up to save the situation. He informed the Duke with the utmost confidence that he should indeed continue his advance. So, in magnificent order, the Guards Brigade and the Highland Brigade marched down to the river, where the Guards in particular waded straight in without considering their personal safety. Once across the Alma, General Bentinck led the Guards Brigade towards the Great Redoubt; first went the Scots Fusilier Guards, then the immaculately aligned Grenadiers and Coldstreams.

General Sir George Brown and Staff.

But they had come too late. Not only was the Great Redoubt an inferno of exploding shells, but advancing on it from the right was a great mass of infantry, four battalions of the Vladimir Regiment, three thousand strong. A scene of remarkable and lamentable confusion ensued. The men of the Light Division, who still held the Great Redoubt, were issued with completely contradictory orders. At first, an unknown voice shouted out, as the Vladimir Regiment strode on, 'The column is French! Don't fire, men! For God's sake don't fire!' Most of the troops obeyed this completely erroneous instruction, while other officers desperately tried to remedy the mistake. Then a bugle sounded the 'Cease fire', and a little later other bugles began to sound the 'Retire'. As officers and sergeants anxiously debated what to do, the troops defending the Great Redoubt began to slip away, leaving nine hundred of their comrades dead or wounded on the slopes of the hill.

As the Light Division retired they fell back onto the advancing lines of the Guards Brigade amid some confusion. Meanwhile, the massed columns of the Vladimir Regiment had tramped into the Great Redoubt; the allied centre was pinned down by artillery fire from the Causeway; on the right, the French had made no further dramatic progress. Prince Menshikov's position seemed a strong one, and capable of further exploitation. Unfortunately for the Russians, however, their commander was still galloping across their front, and in no position to give the crucial orders that might have swung the battle decisively in their favour.

Lord Raglan, on the other hand, had found himself a remarkable vantage point. Conducting himself throughout with his habitual calm, he insisted that his staff officers and their messengers should do likewise (a lesson he had learnt from the Duke of Wellington). So, dressed in his blue frock-coat, white shirt and black cravat, he had trotted, like a well-bred English country gentleman intent on a day's sport, down towards the Alma. Close to the smoking ruins of Bourliuk he had crossed the river, and had ridden up the slope with Russian snipers' bullets whining past him and his staff. Eventually he reached an unoccupied knoll, half way between the Causeway and the Telegraph Height, and looked down upon the battlefield.

He had a magnificent view. On his left, he saw the Causeway batteries, above them the Russian reserves, the whole of the Kourgané Hill, the Great Redoubt, and further Russian reserves (battalions of the Uglitz Regiment and sailors) beyond the Redoubt. He was eight hundred yards inside the Russian lines, but there were no enemy troops near enough to threaten his position.

Immediately Raglan sent back General Airey to summon General Adam's brigade from the 2nd Division. He also remarked wistfully 'Now if only we had a couple of guns!' Hearing this, Colonel Dickson, of the artillery, rode off to do something effective about it. By the time Dickson had returned with two nine-pounders, however, Raglan and his staff on the knoll had seen the Light Division driven out of the Great Redoubt.

But the two guns were now in position, and with a series of glorious targets within easy range. First they opened fire on the batteries near the Causeway in the valley below them; the third and fourth shots ploughed into the Russian positions, and at once the enemy began to limber up and pull off their guns. Next the British gunners found the range of the Russian reserves in front of them, and began blasting great gaps in their ranks until they too retreated out of sight. Then the nine-pounders tried to find the range of the Vladimir battalions at the Great Redoubt; they were unable to reach them, but their shots were close enough to hold back the Russian troops from descending upon the retreating Light Division and punishing it severely. Finally the two British guns were turned onto the battalions of the Kazan Regiment, which were bearing down on the Light Division, and were soon cutting furrows through the closely packed Russian ranks.

While Lord Raglan and the two guns were winning a respite, and indeed an advantage, for the British troops, the French, to the right, were not capitalising on their earlier success. In fact, Prince Menshikov's spontaneous advance with eight battalions to head off the French menace on the seaboard flank of the battle had thrown the French commanders into some confusion.

It was to remedy this situation that a breathless French aide-de-camp was dispatched helter-skelter to beg Lord Raglan for assistance. The apparently unruffled British staff waited patiently until the French officer regained sufficient composure to deliver his message. At last the Frenchman was able to gasp 'My Lord, My Lord, we have before us eight battalions.' 'I can give you one battalion', replied Lord Raglan reasonably, speaking in French. The aide-de-camp then galloped back with his good news, but in fact the British battalion was not eventually required, since the arrival of Canrobert's guns was sufficient to hold back the eight Russian battalions.

The climax of the battle had now been reached. The remarkably effective shooting of the two nine-pounders had cleared the way for a general advance along the British sector of the front. De Lacy Evans' 2nd Division and Sir Richard England's reserve 3rd Division were now able to advance to the relief of the struggling Light Division. The Guards Brigade also pressed forward in immaculate order towards the Vladimir Regiment and the Great and Lesser Redoubts, while further to the left the Highland Brigade began climbing the eastern slopes of the Kourgané Hill which were held by the Susdal battalions.

As the Guards marched towards their objective, coolly opening their ranks 'as if in Hyde Park' to let through stragglers from the Light Division, General Codrington was trying to rally some three hundred men of that division under the colours of the Royal Welsh Fusiliers. Codrington at first thought it would be sensible to form up his fusiliers on the left flank of the advancing Grenadiers, but then, remembering the extraordinary pride of that élitist regiment, asked some of their officers if they would mind marching with a line regiment tagged on to their left. Yes, came the reply, they would mind, so the Grenadiers strode purposefully on, with an embarrassingly wide gap in their left.

But when the Guards approached the Great Redoubt, large numbers of Russian troops swarmed on to the parapet walls and fired into the approaching units with deadly effect. Then a great mass of Russian infantry charged with their bayonets at the Scots Guards; though disinclined to do so, the Scots Guards obeyed urgent orders to fall back, and were harried until they reached the river line. The Guards had lost 171 officers and men killed or wounded, and a great hole had been torn in the middle of their formation.

Seeing the Guards' temporary confusion, Prince Gorchakov led two battalions from the Russian 14th Division in a menacing bayonet charge between the gap in the brigade's lines. Just at that crucial moment an unidentified officer rode up and ordered the Grenadiers, then the Coldstreams, to retire. 'Retire!' demanded Colonel Percy of the Grenadiers. 'What the devil can they mean?' Eventually he decided, very sensibly, that 'they must mean "dress back".' The Grenadiers then took up a defensive formation and began to fire with great accuracy into the charging Russian mass. The Minié rifle did sterling work. Prince Gorchakov's horse was shot from under him; the Russians hesitated, and then began to retreat. Hard on their heels came the Guards regiments, until at last they mounted the parapet wall of the Great Redoubt and found it deserted, save for the dead and wounded.

While the Guards broke the Russians before the Great Redoubt, the Highland Brigade, to their left, advanced against eleven fresh enemy battalions. The Highlanders, comprising the Cameron

The doughty Sir Colin Campbell, Commander of the Highland Brigade.

Highlanders, the 93rd Highlanders and the Black Watch, were led by the able, brave and distinguished Sir Colin Campbell. Before they moved off, Campbell told his brigade:

> Now men, you are going into action. Remember this: whoever is wounded – I don't care what his rank is – whoever it is must lie down where he falls till the bandsmen come to attend him. No soldier must go carrying off wounded men. If any soldier does such a thing his name shall be stuck up in his parish church. Don't be in a hurry about firing. Your officers will tell you when to do so. Be steady. Keep silent. Fire low.

The Highland Brigade swept irresistibly round the back of the

Officers of the 42nd Highlanders (the Black Watch).

Great Redoubt, their dark kilts and plumed bonnets lending them a ghostly appearance in the eyes of their Russian opponents. Calmly and intelligently marshalled by Colin Campbell they advanced, firing accurately as they came, until the Russian columns in front of them wailed in despair, broke and fled.

While Prince Menshikov fulminated, the Russians began a general withdrawal, while the British artillery fired repeatedly into their disheartened ranks. Lord Lucan and the British cavalry were desperate to pursue the Russians, and to turn their retreat into a bloody rout, but Lord Raglan thought better of it. Raglan's decision was due in part to his conviction that the cavalry were too hot-headed and reckless to unleash while dusk was falling and while three thousand fresh Russian cavalry lurked somewhere to their left. He had also received a message from the ill and exhausted Marshal St Arnaud telling him that the French could not join with the British in pursuit of the enemy because they had left their knapsacks north of thc Alma and because their artillery had shot off all of its ammunition.

So Lord Raglan ordered his men to bivouac for the night, while the army surgeons lopped off arms and legs, and the hospital transport ships lay waiting to carry the wounded, often filthy and neglected, to the tender mercies of the orderlies at Scutari.

The battle of the Alma was over, the first full-scale battle between European nations since Waterloo. There was no doubt that the allies had won the day, though the French had failed to exploit their unexpected success on the seaboard flank, and the British had been unable to make full capital out of the Russian withdrawal. That the British had been both brave, and bravely led, was indisputable. Moreover, Lord Raglan's use of the line in attack had been successful, though his full frontal assault across the Alma accorded ill with text-book convention. At the cost of two thousand British killed and wounded, and an estimated, but debatable, 1,300 French losses, the Russians had been driven from their chosen defensive position with the loss of over five thousand men. The campaign had begun well.

Chapter 5

The Battle of Balaclava

The allied army, numbering some sixty thousand men, now moved south towards the Russian citadel of Sebastopol. The subsequent manoeuvres have been the subject of much historical debate, and were passionately argued over by the officers of both sides at the time. Many Russian observers believed that if the allies had attacked Sebastopol from the north then the town would have fallen easily. Prince Gorchakov, who had commanded the right wing of the Russian army at the Battle of Alma, later declared 'There was nothing to stop the Allies marching into the town.'

This is an over-simplified view. Sir John Burgoyne, Raglan's chief engineer, considered that the fortifications confronting any advance from the north, though in a state of indifferent repair, were still sufficient to offer a serious obstacle. The French commander St Arnaud, who was now seen to be fatally stricken, also advocated skirting the north side of Sebastopol and attacking the town from the south. The opinions of Burgoyne and St Arnaud prevailed, and soon the allied army, with the British forces in the vanguard, was marching round Sebastopol to the south. This decision was one of the most crucial of the war, since there is strong evidence that an assault from the north would almost certainly have succeeded. Sebastopol would then have fallen, and months of bloody and wasteful siege warfare been averted.

Why did Lord Raglan agree to the flank march round Sebastopol, when he had argued on the day after the Battle of Alma for a rapid assault on the northern forts of the Russian citadel? Perhaps the main reason was that he was excessively anxious to preserve Anglo-French accord, and therefore deferred, much against his better judgement, to the French point of view. Also Raglan's consistent politeness and consideration all too frequently served to mask his real opinions. Thus St Arnaud seems to have been genuinely unaware of Raglan's desire to push on as hard and as soon as possible after the Alma. For his part, the stricken French commander complained that his troops were tired, that the next river, the Katcha, was a formidable obstacle, and that the one after that, the Belbek, was very strongly defended.

Opposite The charge of the Light Brigade.

Lord Raglan could hardly march on without the French. He needed their numbers for one thing, since the British regiments had lost two thousand of their finest troops on the Alma. Particularly because he saw himself as responsible for maintaining an amicable understanding with the French, he was conscious that some of his officers were irritated by the extravagant claims made by some of their French counterparts, who were talking as if they had won the Battle of the Alma singlehanded. St Arnaud was similarly convinced that he had already covered himself with military glory, though such hyperbole is perhaps forgivable in a dying man. At any rate, he wrote home to his wife, 'Victory! Victory! Yesterday I beat the Russians completely. I took their formidable positions which were defended by forty thousand men. They fought bravely but nothing could resist the impetuosity of the French.'

On 22 September the allied armies had still not stirred from the Alma, since the French would not agree to an advance. Lord Raglan therefore availed himself of the hiatus in order to bury the British dead and to ensure that the wounded were properly attended to and taken back to the ships. Since, despite the French claims, the British had lost considerably more men than their allies this melancholy process took some time, and soon St Arnaud was unjustifiably complaining that 'they have more wounded than me', but 'the English are not ready yet'.

At last on 23 September both armies set out under a warm sun. The troops were able to filch and plunder as they marched, taking grapes, melons, onions, apricots and an odd hen or two. As they passed occasional grand houses these, too, were robbed, and china, ornaments and utensils added to the army's loot. Morale was high, and the cholera seemed to have abated.

On 24 September the river Belbek was crossed and, mounting the far side of the valley, the army caught its first sight of Sebastopol with its sparkling white buildings and copper domes. St Arnaud, who was now so ill that he could not confer with Lord Raglan, opted out of the discussion of what to do. Raglan still favoured an attack from the north, to synchronise with a naval bombardment from the south. If this were done, he anticipated an early capture of the formidable Star Fort to the north of the city and a relatively easy advance thereafter.

Sir John Burgoyne, Raglan's Chief Engineer, by D. J. Pound.

Sir John Burgoyne (the illegitimate son of the General Burgoyne who had surrendered so disastrously at Saratoga during the American War of Independence) thought differently. Raglan's chief engineer argued that an attack from the south would contain the important element of surprise, and would in addition be directed against imperfect defences. Moreover, to the south of Sebastopol lay the port of Balaclava which would provide the allies with an apparently convenient harbour. Raglan now became convinced that it was too late to attack effectively from the north, and that the French, like Burgoyne, were committed to an assault from the south.

Lord Cardigan,
by De Prades.

The Thin Red Line,
by Robert Gibb.

Robert Gibb /81

Lord Lucan, Commander of the Cavalry Division at the Battle of Balaclava. *Below* Balaclava, by Lady Butler.

Thus, on 25 September, the flank march continued. The Russians meanwhile had not been idle. Prince Menshikov had forced Admiral Kornilov to scuttle his fleet in Sebastopol harbour rather than confront the allied warships in the Black Sea. The Russian commander also made the important decision to send the major part of his army out of Sebastopol towards Bakchi Serai to the north-east; by so doing he hoped to offer a serious threat to the landwards flank of the allied armies. Indeed as Lord Raglan led his forces southwards, Lord Lucan and the cavalry came upon the rearguard of a vast Russian column marching north-eastwards past Mackenzie's Farm (named after an earlier Scottish settler in the Crimea). Raglan called off the British cavalry before they could make an all-out assault on the Russian army, though they did manage to snatch some supply wagons loaded with such variegated booty as food, wigs, coarse brandy, women's underclothes and pornographic novels written in French.

By nightfall on 25 September the British army was spread out from the river Chernaya to the Belbek. While Lord Raglan's staff feasted off the roast leg of a wild boar which had been shot and presented to them, the Commander-in-Chief himself was beset with anxiety; 'We were', he subsequently wrote, 'in a dangerous situation.' Certainly his army was wide open to a surprise attack in a barely reconnoitred countryside and cut off from the fleet which was still anchored at the mouth of the Katcha.

But next morning the army stirred itself under a benign sun, and, well-rested and breakfasted, struck out for the fishing-village and summer resort of Balaclava. After pushing aside some ineffective mortar fire, the British forces entered Balaclava, where local people held up trays piled high with fruit, flowers and bread as a sign of friendship.

The French arrived the next day (27 September) and General Canrobert, who had now taken over from St Arnaud, discussed with Lord Raglan the positions to be taken up by the allied armies. It was obvious that the disappointingly narrow, land-locked harbour of Balaclava could not serve as a supply base for both armies. Raglan, wrongly advised by Rear-Admiral Sir Edmund Lyons, chose to remain at Balaclava, while the French went to the better facilities of the two western bays of Kamiesh and Kazach. This decision was to place an enormous strain on the British forces, for not only did they have to make use of an inadequate base, but they were also committed to defending the land flank of the allied forces from attack at the same time as laying siege to Sebastopol itself.

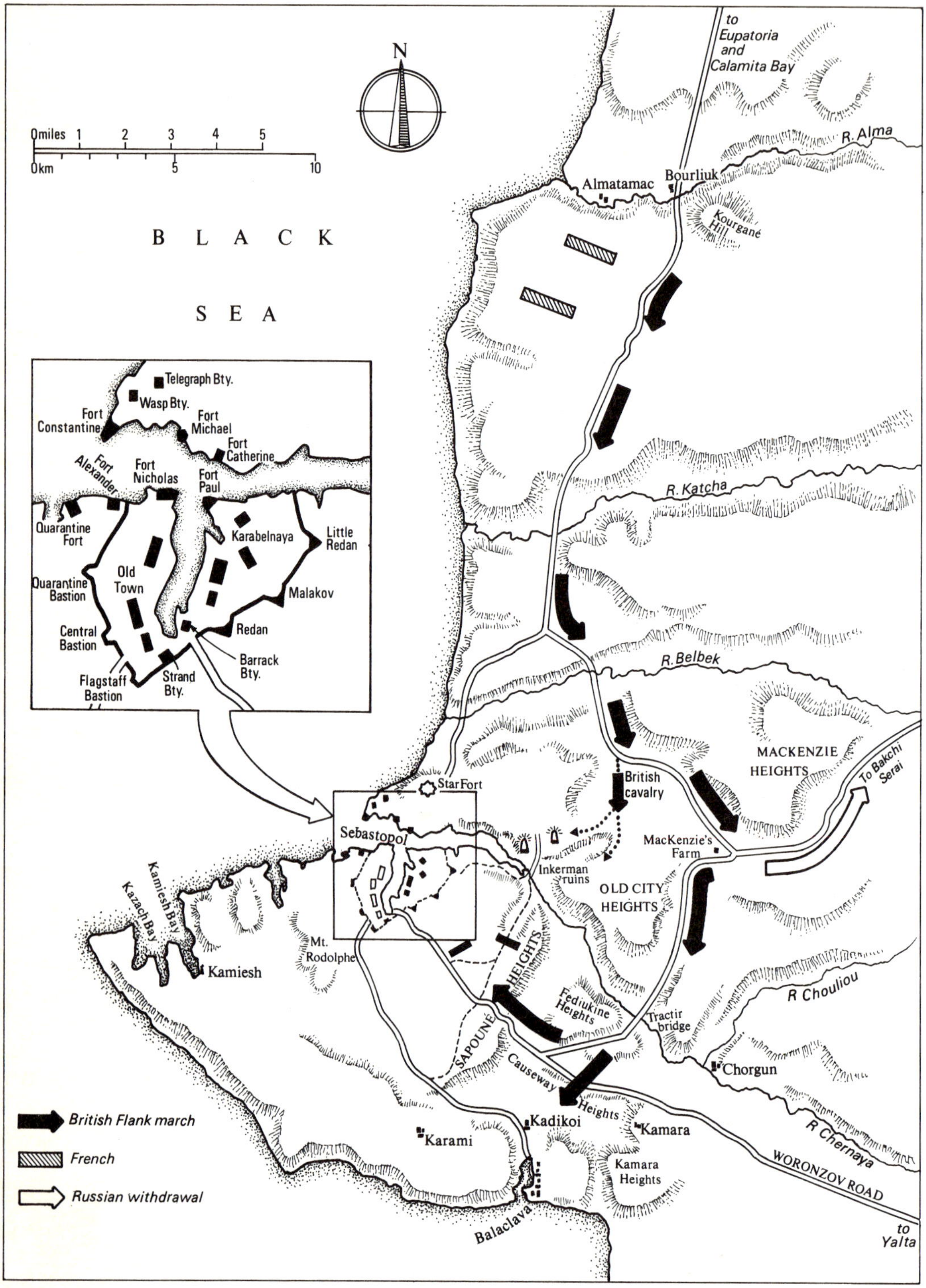

The march to
Sebastopol from the
Alma.

When Lord Raglan made the decision to hold on to Balaclava he did not, of course, anticipate a protracted siege. Indeed between 27 September and 10 October Raglan still pressed for an immediate assault on Sebastopol. But he was unable to convince either Canrobert or Sir John Burgoyne of the wisdom of this course. Burgoyne argued that the defences of Sebastopol must first be reduced by a heavy artillery bombardment; Canrobert, a brave, popular and highly professional officer, would not risk a direct assault over open ground and with the possibility of a flank attack from Menshikov's army to the north-east.

Sir George Cathcart, commander of the 4th Division, shared Raglan's view that an early attack would have been successful, and wrote 'I am sure I could walk into it, with scarcely the loss of a man, at night or an hour before daybreak ... we could leave our packs and run into it even in open day, only risking a few shots while we passed the redoubt. We see people walking about the streets in great consternation.'

Caution, however, prevailed. By 10 October it was evident that the allies had decided to submit Sebastopol to a formal siege. Sir George Cathcart had known of Lord Raglan's costly decision by the evening of 28 September, and had expostulated, 'Land the siege-trains! But, my dear Lord Raglan, what the devil is there to knock down?'

With every day that passed, however, there was indeed more and more to knock down. Two men worked to the limits of their skill and strength to inspire the garrison and citizens of Sebastopol and to improve the fortifications of the town. One was Admiral Kornilov, whose fleet lay scuttled in Sebastopol harbour, but who now flung himself into the task of inspiring, with God's help, an heroic resistance to the invaders. His ubiquitous enthusiasm was all the more necessary in view of the fact that Prince Menshikov was still some considerable distance from Sebastopol with the bulk of the army.

The second bulwark of the defences of Sebastopol was Lieutenant-Colonel Todleben, who was about to win undying fame as an engineer of genius. Tirelessly Todleben sited guns, ordered ramparts to be thrown up, and strengthened existing fortifications. There were six main redoubts on the perimeters of Sebastopol: the Quarantine Bastion (nearest to the sea on the west), the Central Bastion, the Flagstaff Bastion, the Redan, the Malakov, and the Little Redan. The Russians worked desperately at these defences, as well as making quite frequent and successful sallies against the advancing allies. They were also being steadily reinforced by forces

A later portrait of General Todleben, the Russian engineer who so successfully defended Sebastopol, by D. J. Pound.

drawn from Odessa and other conveniently situated bases. By 9 October twenty-eight thousand fresh troops had entered Sebastopol, and the garrison numbered about thirty-eight thousand in all.

By the second week in October, therefore, the Russians had fully recovered their balance after their defeat on the Alma. The allies, for their part, had frittered away their early advantage in prevarication and disagreement; French élan had been little in evidence, and Lord Raglan's constant and accommodating politeness had been a poor substitute for an intelligent and unbending resolve.

The main hope of the allies now lay in pounding the Russian defences to fragments under a shattering bombardment. After much travail the heavy guns and siege equipment were hauled onto the plateau outside Sebastopol, and nearby wooden houses ripped to pieces to provide gun platforms suitable for the rocky terrain. The preparations were painfully slow, and a British officer wrote home despairingly, 'They call it a siege. It's more like garden digging. We shan't get anywhere like this.'

At last, on 17 October at 6.30 am the cannonade began. The Russians had meanwhile been able to increase the number of their guns on the landward side of Sebastopol from 172 to 341. Against them the allies had assembled 126 guns of which 53 were French and 73 British. Of the 53 French guns, 49 were sited on Mount Rodolphe facing the Central Bastion.

A naval bombardment had been planned to coordinate with the

land cannonade, but it was dogged by misfortune. The Anglo-French warships were due to open fire at the same time as the land guns, but on the evening of 16 October the French Admiral Hamelin informed Admiral Dundas that he would be unable to begin firing until 10.30 the next morning because 'his shot would not last long and, if expended early, the enemy might think that he was beaten off'. Dundas accepted this change of plan, but was staggered to receive the news on the morning of 17 October, after the land bombardment had begun, that the French wanted to alter the plan again.

This time Hamelin told Dundas that, on the orders of Canrobert himself, the allied fleets should now be anchored in line to deliver their broadsides, not allowed freedom of manoeuvre. Dundas pointed out that the lines proposed were too far away from the Russian fortifications to do serious damage, but the French were adamant, and the British admiral gave way.

It was well into the afternoon before the fleets opened fire against the hard limestone forts. The bombardment was an impressive sight as over 1,100 guns blazed away at the Russian defences. But the cannonade had little effect; the forts were scarcely damaged save for Fort Constantine, and in reply the Russian guns wreaked havoc amongst the anchored wooden warships. When the action was broken off at 5.30 pm, the Royal Navy had lost three hundred men either killed or wounded, and at least seven British warships had suffered serious damage.

The land bombardment was going much better, even though a French magazine on Mount Rodolphe was blown sky-high, causing the batteries to cease firing for the day. But the British guns did considerable damage, and reduced the Redan to rubble. The French, however, were not prepared to assault the defences of Sebastopol, and next morning the Russians had effected remarkable repairs to their fortifications. This dispiriting pattern was repeated over several days: a successful bombardment, a failure to launch an attack, nightfall, and extraordinary Russian repairs carried out under cover of darkness. Yet Russian losses were heavy, over two thousand killed during the first three days of the cannonade, and including, on 17 October, the inspired Admiral Kornilov.

But on 24 October the allies had their attention dramatically diverted from Sebastopol, for behind them to the north-east Prince Menshikov was assembling an army under General Liprandi, supported by General Jabrokritski, on the Chernaya river. The Russian intention was to cut the vital Woronzov road connecting Balaclava to Sebastopol, and to threaten Balaclava itself.

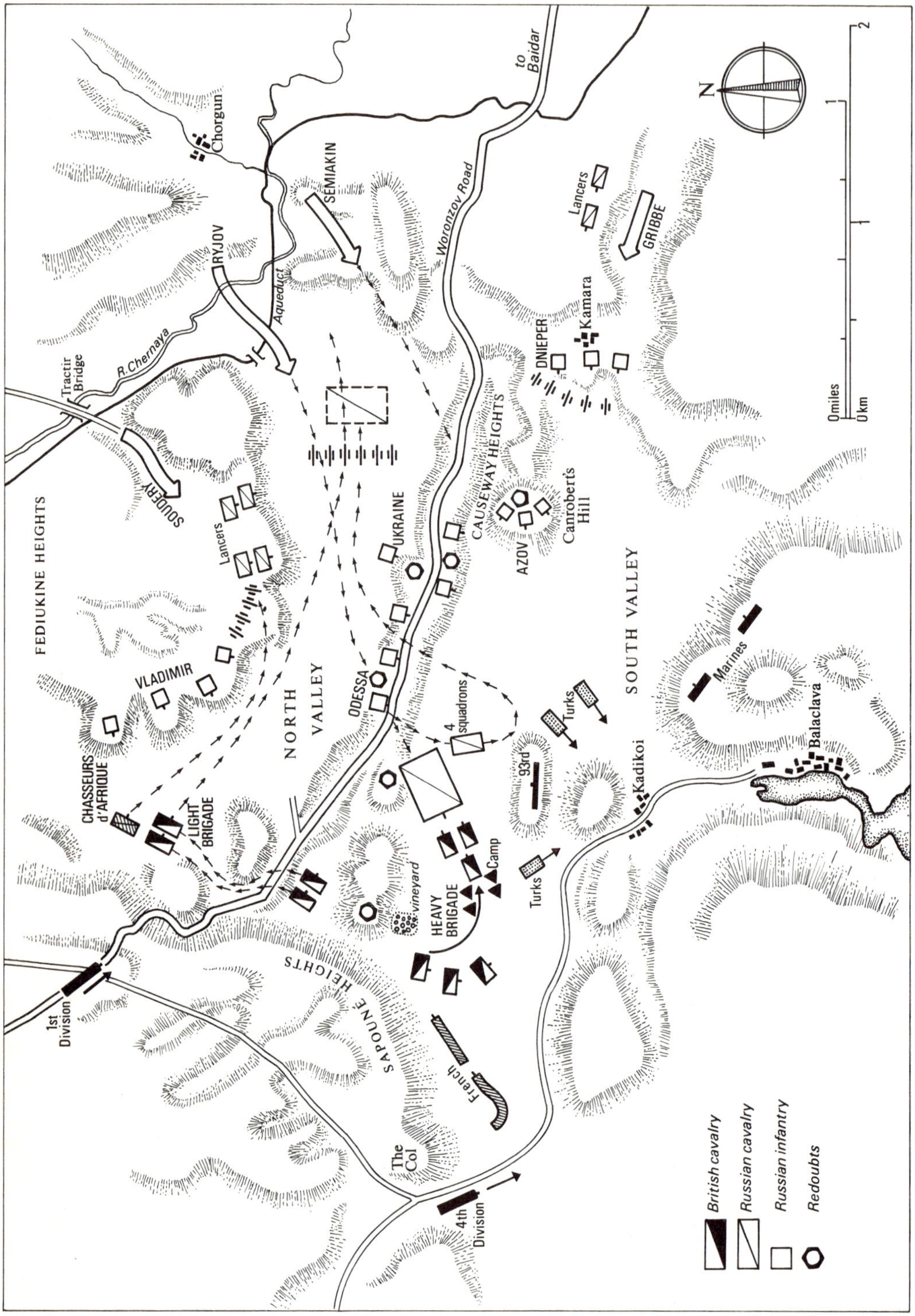

The Battle of Balaclava.

On 25 October the Russian army of twenty-five thousand foot, thirty-four squadrons of horse, and seventy-eight guns advanced towards Balaclava. The allied forces were drawn up in the following order: the French on the left flank, and the British on the right; some Turkish detachments manning the redoubts on the Causeway Heights which protected Balaclava.

The Russians pushed on, and achieved early success in the centre by overrunning the foremost Turkish outposts. But then, in the Fediukine Valley, they found themselves confronted by the 93rd Highland Regiment and the British cavalry, led by Lucan. The 93rd, inspired by their commander the doughty Sir Colin Campbell with the words 'Remember there is no retreat. You must die where you stand!' did indeed stand firm, and turned aside the Russian cavalry. In so doing they inspired *The Times* correspondent, W. H. Russell, to describe them as a 'thin red streak topped with steel'. Thus originated the much quoted phrase the 'thin red line': it was a description born out of heroism, but also the result of unpreparedness – since it was standard military practice to arrange infantry about to receive cavalry either in squares or in lines four deep. The speed and success of the Russian advance was, more than anything else, responsible for the formation of the 'thin red line' at Balaclava.

The 93rd could not, however, check the Russian assault single-handed. This task fell to Lucan's cavalry. The Heavy Brigade, led by General Sir James Scarlett, and consisting of six squadrons, dressed their lines immaculately despite Lucan's repeated orders to charge. The three thousand Russian cavalry that were pouring over the Causeway Heights halted at the sight of this parade ground display. It seemed absurd that the gaudily dressed British squadrons, numbering a mere eight hundred men, could stop the Russians, sombre and businesslike in their yellowish-grey overcoats.

At last when Scarlett was satisfied that his ranks were in proper order, he turned and led the charge at the enemy who stood 'as if fascinated, unable to move'. In a flurry of hooves and flashing sabre blades the Scots Greys, the Inniskilling Dragoons and the Dragoon Guards crashed into the Russian centre. Such a mass of men were milling and jostling and cursing at the point of impact that the British cavalrymen, hardly able to use their swords in the text-book fashion, hacked at their opponents as if wielding meat-cleavers. After five minutes of desperate fighting the Russian ranks began to waver; their discomfiture was heightened by some British artillery fire falling upon their rear. After eight minutes the Russians broke and fled over the Causeway Heights.

The Heavy Brigade had won an amazing victory against odds of nearly four to one. The troopers' sword arms were weary from hacking and thrusting. Sir James Scarlett had received five sabre cuts, and his dashing aide-de-camp, Lieutenant Elliott, fourteen! Lord Raglan, who was observing the battle from higher ground, sent a simple but appropriate message, 'Well done, Scarlett.'

The commander of the Light Brigade, Lord Cardigan, who was also watching the fighting from a mere five hundred yards up the valley, commented with a mixture of envy and petulance 'Damn those Heavies, they have the laugh of us this day.' He need not have feared for within a matter of minutes he was to lead one of the most celebrated cavalry charges in British history.

General Scarlett, Commander of the Heavy Brigade.

The charge of the Light Brigade at Balaclava became the best remembered incident of the whole Crimean War, nobly assisted in its rise to public acclaim by Alfred Tennyson's verses and generations of subsequent cramming in board schools and public schools alike. In military terms, however, the charge was one of the least useful or important assaults of the campaign. Its immediate effects were futile, its long-term advantages dubious.

Still, there it is, exerting, even after the passage of more than a century, a fascination over the imagination and providing the material for endless academic debate. It is the classical example of military confusion and ineptitude, infused at the same time with matchless heroism, dash and determination. Some disentangling of the fateful events which led to the charge of the Light Brigade is necessary.

As Lord Cardigan sat at the head of his 673 men watching the triumph of the Heavy Brigade upon the Causeway Heights his officers were beside themselves with impatience. As the Russian cavalry broke up in confusion, the junior officer temporarily commanding the 17th Lancers rode up to Cardigan and said:

'My Lord, are you not going to charge the flying enemy?'

'No,' replied Cardigan. 'We have orders to remain here.'

'But, my Lord, it is our positive duty to follow up this advantage.'

'No,' said Cardigan. 'We must remain here.'

'Do, my Lord,' insisted Captain Morris, 'Do allow me to charge them with the 17th. Sir, my Lord, they are in disorder.'

'No, no sir!' snapped Cardigan.

Cardigan afterwards asserted that Lord Lucan's instructions did not enable him to advance at this point in the battle. Lord Lucan, on the other hand, claimed that he had already empowered Cardigan to take advantage of any reasonable opportunity to attack. At any rate, the Light Brigade made no move. Lord Raglan was by now convinced that Cardigan's fresh squadrons should be sent in to hammer home the victory won by the Heavy Brigade. Unfortunately the infantry support that such an attack theoretically required was not forthcoming, though troops of the 1st Division were moving slowly towards the valley, and Sir George Cathcart's 4th Division had actually been ordered to advance and capture the redoubts from which the Russians had so recently been driven.

Raglan therefore decided to use the Light Brigade unsupported by infantry. He had little choice but to do so. Lord Lucan had ignored an order issued nearly an hour earlier stating 'Cavalry to advance and take advantage of any opportunity to recover the Heights. They will be supported by the infantry, which have been ordered to advance on two fronts.' There was still no infantry in evidence, and Lord Lucan thus continued to hold his men in check.

While waiting on events, Raglan's staff suddenly saw that Russian horse artillerymen were trying to tow away the abandoned guns on the Heights. A specific new order was now composed. It read: 'Lord Raglan wishes the cavalry to advance rapidly to the front – follow the enemy and try to prevent the enemy carrying away the guns. Troop Horse Artillery may accompany. French cavalry is on your left. Immediate.'

Captain Lewis Nolan was the staff officer chosen to deliver this fateful message. Nolan was selected probably because he was a superb horseman and could ride rapidly down the steep descent into the valley below. In other respects, however, he was far from being the ideal messenger: he was excitable, conceited and priggish, and he openly despised both Lucan and Cardigan. Nolan handed Lucan the order. The cavalry commander read its contents slowly and with mounting consternation, then announced that such an attack would be 'useless'. The fuming Nolan replied: 'Lord Raglan's orders are that the cavalry should attack immediately.'

'Attack, sir!' countered Lucan. 'Attack what? What guns, sir? Where and what to do?'

Nolan waved his arm in a contemptuous gesture down the valley. 'There, my Lord. There is the enemy! There are your guns!'

Lord Lucan was not short-sighted, but, denied Lord Raglan's lofty vantage point, all he could see were attended Russian guns massed at the further end of the valley. He rode over to Cardigan and ordered him to advance. Even Cardigan, moustachios bristling, spoiling for a fight, hesitated.

'Certainly, sir,' he replied. 'But allow me to point out to you that the Russians have a battery in the valley in our front, and batteries and riflemen on each flank.'

'I know it,' said Lucan. 'But Lord Raglan will have it. We have no choice but to obey.'

Cardigan turned towards his men, murmuring, 'Well, here goes the last of the Brudenells!' He then gave the order to advance. As the men of the Light Brigade trotted down the valley, Captain Nolan, who had stayed to take part in the charge, suddenly dashed before Cardigan, waving his sword and shrieking at him. Probably he realised that the cavalry were heading towards the manned guns, not towards the Causeway Heights, and was trying to avert disaster. Whatever his motives they brought him a violent death, for a splinter from an exploding Russian shell tore into his chest and killed him.

Captain Nolan, the bearer of the fateful message to charge the guns at Balaclava.

From various positions, the allied troops looked on with horror as the Light Brigade was steadily shot to pieces. A torrent of artillery and musket fire poured into their ranks from three sides of the valley. Cardigan rode at the centre, crying 'Close in! Close in! Do look to your dressing on the left!' On every hand his men toppled about him, bodies mutilated, limbs blown off, their horses disembowelled. Eventually the decimated front rank of the British advance reached the Russian guns, and hacked at any of the enemy still in sight. Then, seeing the Russian cavalry drawn up

Charge of the Light
Brigade, Balaclava,
25 October 1854.

Valley of the Shadow of Death, 1855 (Fenton).

behind the guns, Cardigan turned and trotted back, furious with Captain Nolan's insolence and determined to lodge a complaint.

But even then it was not over. The remaining lines of the Light Brigade broke through past the guns and, seeing at last that they were hopelessly outnumbered, wheeled round and retreated. Of the 673 men who took part in the charge (or trot), 113 were killed and 134 wounded, nearly five hundred horses were destroyed, and the gorgeous uniforms of this élitist brigade were besmirched with dirt and soaked in blood.

The charge of the Light Brigade was, of course, a disaster: splendid, heroic, but grotesquely contravening standard military practice. Compared with later losses sustained by British forces, during the Great War, for example, the death of 113 out of 673 does not seem excessive. The fame or notoriety of the assault owes much more to the confusion over the order transmitted from Lord Raglan via Captain Nolan. Lord Raglan can hardly be blamed for this. Nor, in a sense, can Lords Lucan and Cardigan, though both (especially Lucan) could have exercised more discretion – after all, there were several examples of straightforward refusals to obey orders during the campaign. Nolan, unfortunately, could bear no witness.

Raglan was incensed at the catastrophe, but tried to shield Lucan from official criticism. Cardigan was quite unrepentant, and rode from the field of battle to take a bath, consume a bottle of champagne, and go to bed. It was not long before he left the Crimea at his own request. Lucan was simply recalled.

The final tragedy of the wasteful yet heroic charge of the Light Brigade was that it did nothing to win the battle and, arguably, lost it. The Russian advance on Balaclava had been halted. But they still occupied the Causeway Heights, and commanded the vital Woronzov road, possession of which would have allowed the British to move supplies easily from Balaclava and would have thus averted some of the horrors of the coming winter.

Chapter 6

Inkerman: 'The Soldiers' Battle'

The day after the battle of Balaclava, 26 October, the Russians launched a minor offensive against the British 2nd Division positioned on the Home Ridge (over which ran the post road from Inkerman Bridge towards the Woronzov Road). Colonel Federov, with six battalions (about five thousand men) and four guns, broke through the outlying British positions but was turned back by artillery fire from Home Ridge. The Russians lost some 270 killed and wounded in this battle of 'Little Inkerman', and the British about a hundred. But the commander of the 2nd Division, Sir George de Lacy Evans, was hurt by a fall from his horse and handed over to Brigadier-General Pennefather of the 1st Brigade, who led the division in the subsequent battle of Inkerman.

That evening there was more reshuffling of senior positions when Lord Raglan received a letter from the Duke of Newcastle (the Secretary of State for War) which informed him that the government had decided that Sir George Cathcart should give up his 'dormant commission' to succeed to the command of the army in the event of Raglan's death. Raglan was relieved to have the matter cleared up, for he claimed that it had disturbed his normally close relationship with Sir George Brown, the most senior of his divisional commanders. Cathcart expressed his relief as well, but within ten days he was killed in action at Inkerman.

The siege of Sebastopol continued in the aftermath of Balaclava. The heavy guns pounded the town's defences, but it seemed to some observers that the more punishment they took the stronger the defences became.

The allied armies now began to experience the onset of winter. There was a good deal of rain, and sharp-edged winds. The army began to doubt whether it would storm Sebastopol at all. As the men huddled miserably in their trenches, a British infantry sergeant wrote to his parents:

Opposite Death of General Sir George Cathcart at Inkerman.

> We had a rough 24 hours of it. It rained nearly the whole time. The enemy kept pitching shells into us nearly all night and it took all our time to dodge their Whistling Dicks [large Russian shells that made a curious whirring noise]. We were standing nearly all night; the cold, bleak wind cutting through our thin clothing (that now is getting very thin and full of holes, and nothing to mend it with). This is ten times worse than all the fighting ... We have not one ounce too much to eat ... We are nearly worked to death night and day. We cannot move without sinking nearly to our ankles in mud. The tents we have to sleep in are full of holes, and there is nothing but mud to lie down in ... I suppose we shall have leather medals for this one day – I mean those

who have the good fortune to escape the shot and shell of the enemy and the pestilence that surrounds us.

Lord Raglan continued at first to be popular enough with his troops, though he was extraordinarily reluctant to show himself to them, to acknowledge their cheers, or even to say a few trite words of encouragement. His diffidence and his dislike of emotional display, though fine, stoical qualities in themselves, were quite inappropriate to the task of keeping morale high, and it was predictable that soon the men were grumbling that because Lord Raglan chose not to come among them he could have no accurate idea of their hardships and sufferings.

Of course Raglan was a deeply preoccupied man. Sebastopol had not fallen; he had lost too many good troops through battle and disease; the French were not the most cooperative of allies; winter was closing in. Yet he was apparently incapable of forcibly spelling out his difficulties to his political masters in Whitehall. His letters to the Duke of Newcastle and others were studied exercises in understatement. Perhaps the chief reason for this was his desire to shield the home government from the embarrassment of shrill appeals for help and gloomy accounts of his misfortunes. Certainly his Quartermaster-General, Airey, believed this, and told a post-war Board of Inquiry so in uncompromising terms:

> Men went to him anxious and perturbed. They came away firm. By a like happy ascendancy he sheltered the home authorities from the dangers of undue apprehension. He knew that their fears would rapidly spread panic in England, and that panic in England would be injurious to the efficiency of the forces. Yet he did not conceal – he carefully denoted – the wants of the Army, and it is singular that he should find words to do so effectually without creating alarm …
>
> It is possible that – by one unaccustomed to military affairs – the true import and consequence of the facts thus conveyed would have been more completely understood if the narrative had been given in that form of lamentation which can be appropriately adopted by civilians when labouring under heavy trials. But it was not well that that should be, and perhaps too, it may be confessed that against such a way of writing and speaking, Lord Raglan had a soldier's prejudice.

Another source of concern to Lord Raglan, and indeed to the whole army, was the uninhibited reporting of *The Times* and other newspapers. Raglan did not attempt to censor Russell's reports for *The Times*, even when they became bitterly critical of him personally, though he did try to get the Duke of Newcastle to speak to the editor in London. He did not object to legitimate criticism; what he found intolerable was the printing of military secrets.

Certainly *The Times*' description of the army's dispositions, including its weak points in strategy and supply, were potentially very useful to the enemy. It was, moreover, reckoned by the rueful British officers that the newspaper reached Sebastopol before it reached Balaclava, and the Tsar was reported as saying 'We have no need of spies, we have *The Times*.' An irate officer of the Royal Fusiliers was quite convinced that 'that blackguard Russell' was responsible for increasing the hazards to be faced:

> The Russians left off shooting at our camp entirely but Mr Russell must needs go put in his paper that the balls had reached us. We saw it in *The Times* a fortnight ago and at the moment I saw it I said that as soon as the Russians heard it we should be shot at again, and sure enough the night before last just as we were at dinner they commenced their evening's performance. Russell takes precious care to live about a mile out of range.

The Russians, however, did not need *The Times* to tell them that the British defensive positions guarding the approaches to Balaclava were vulnerable. They had, after all, tested the weakest point of the line with their sortie against the 2nd Division on 26 October. For the next week the Russians built up their strength in the Chernaya valley. Prince Menshikov had about 120,000 men at his disposal; the British a mere twenty-five thousand fit troops, and the French forty thousand.

Despite the fact that the initiative now seemed to have passed to the Russians, and despite the ominous menace of 'Little Inkerman', no new dispositions were made on the British front. The 2nd Division were still encamped on Home Ridge; of the 1st Division, the Guards Brigade was near to the windmill on the post road, while the Highland Brigade was at Balaclava; the camps of the 3rd and 4th Divisions stretched away to the west of the windmill; the remnants of the Light Brigade were in support of the Guards' position, and the Heavy Brigade was encamped near Lord Raglan's Headquarters on the col to the left of the post road and at the eastern end of the Wellway gully.

The geography of the battle area should now be described in view of the piecemeal and isolated conflicts that characterised the subsequent engagement. Inkerman Ridge rose sharply and massively from the south bank of the river Chernaya; this heavily wooded spur contained ridges as high as 636 feet above sea level (Home Ridge for example), and averaged about four hundred feet overall. To the south-west it was bounded by the Careenage Ravine, which divided it from the parallel Victoria Ridge; out of the Careenage Ravine ran two gullies, the Mikriakov and the Wellway.

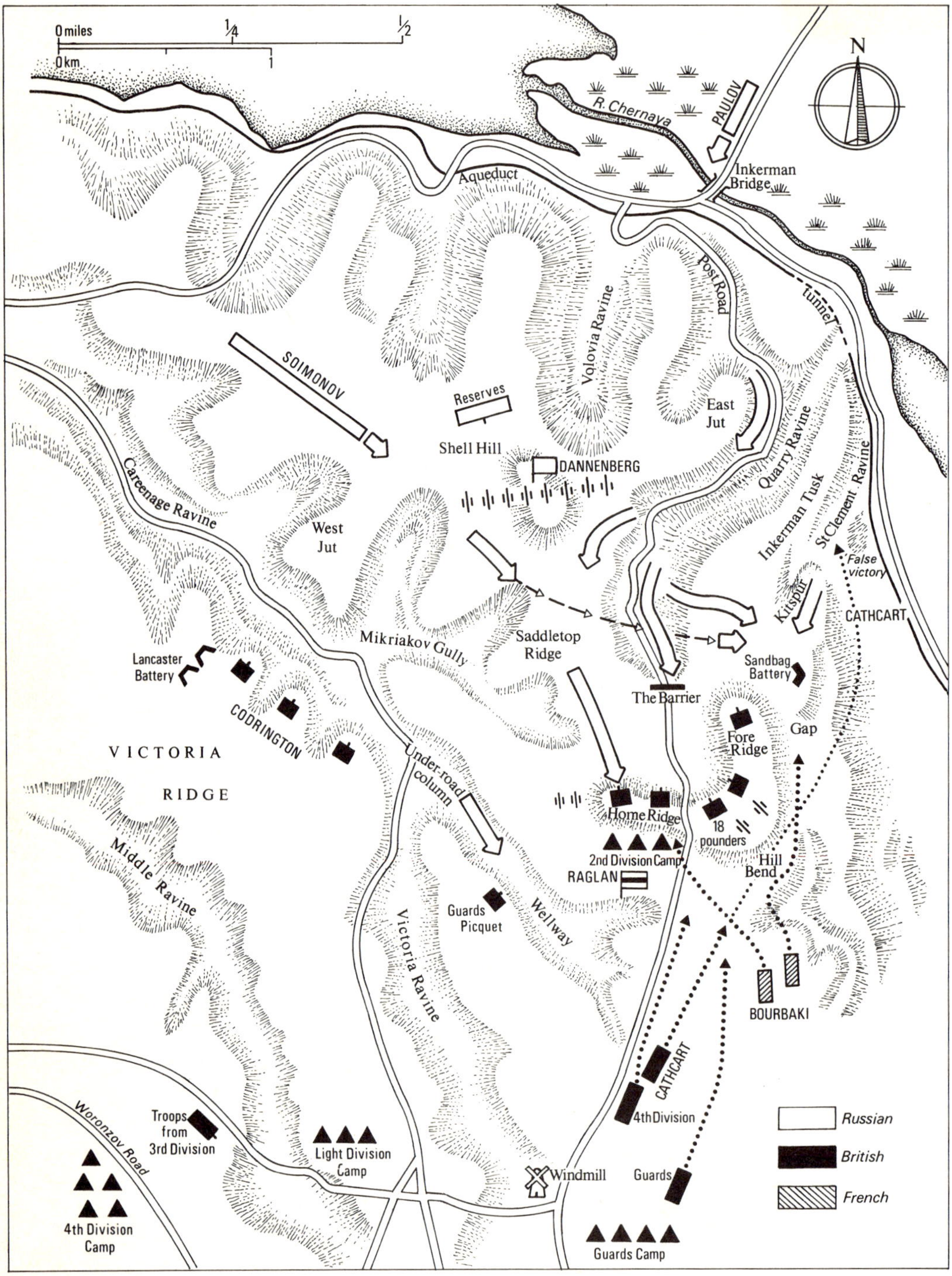

The Battle of Inkerman.

Troops marching along the strategically vital Woronzov Road.

To the north-east of Inkerman Ridge there were three similar gullies leading to the main British position on Home Ridge: the Volovia, Quarry and St Clement Ravines; of these the Quarry Ravine was the most important, for along it ran the post road from Inkerman Bridge (over the Chernaya) to the south. In the middle of the south-eastern end of Inkerman Ridge was the Shell Hill, to the south of which was the British 2nd Division.

The Russian tactics were straightforward. They planned to attack and defeat the British army, while pinning down the French who were stationed on the Sapouné Heights on the right flank of the

The Rifle Brigade at Inkerman, by Orlando Norrie.

British. To achieve this, General Soimonov was to advance from Sebastopol with an army of nineteen thousand men along Inkerman Ridge until he established his artillery to the west of Shell Hill; General Paulov's army of sixteen thousand men was to descend from the Mackenzie Heights, cross the Inkerman Bridge, and then advance along the Quarry Ravine and take up position

to the east of Shell Hill. General Gorchakov, with twenty-two thousand men, was meanwhile to demonstrate against the French on the Sapouné Heights.

As soon as Soimonov's and Paulov's forces had linked up on Shell Hill, General Dannenberg was to assume command and drive south over Home Ridge and towards the windmill at the junction of the post road and the Woronzov Road. At this point, Gorchakov was to attack from the east and help crush the British army in a pincer movement.

Apart from the destruction of the British army, the Russian high command also hoped to divert the French from their impending attack on the Flagstaff Bastion, preparations for which were nearly complete. In fact, the French attack was scheduled for the night of 7 November. But by 3 November the allied commanders were aware that the Russians were about to launch a new offensive against them. Not only had the Grand Dukes Nicholas and

Pte P. Maguire 33rd Foot escaping from the Russians at Inkerman, by M. A. Hayes.

Michael arrived in Sebastopol to watch the expected Russian triumph, but two divisions of Dannenberg's 4th Corps had also come from Odessa, thus completing the Russian reinforcements. Oddly, the news of the impending attack had leaked out in Europe, where London and Paris apparently knew more about the Russian plans than Raglan and Canrobert, the men on the spot.

The Russians began to move into the offensive at 2 am on Sunday 5 November. The previous day the Tsar had spent three hours in his private chapel praying for the success of his armies in the coming battle. Certainly the god of weather, if not the god of battles, answered these royal prayers from St Petersburg, for a persistent rain fell during the night before the attack making the British outposts less alert than usual; the rumbling of Russian gun carriages was in fact heard, but dismissed by British sentries as coming from supply wagons. In any case, who would think of launching a major attack under such a downpour? As dawn broke at about 4 am the rain eased, but was replaced by dense mist. The Russian preparations were thus effectively shielded from their enemies.

General Codrington, of the Light Division, had been on his horse before dawn, visiting the outposts of his brigade. As he rode along Victoria Ridge (which was parallel to Inkerman Ridge) he became aware of muffled noises and movements to the front. Suddenly he heard a burst of firing to the left of the Light Division's position. Realising that the army had been caught unaware, Codrington galloped back to rouse the Light Division for action.

Now the British pickets on the forward slopes of Inkerman Ridge were able to make out the vast Russian columns looming up out of the mist, as Soimonov's army approached from Sebastopol and Paulov's from the north. Dannenberg had in fact ordered Soimonov to march along the Victoria Ridge, but the latter ignored these instructions and stuck to the original plan; it is quite possible that if Soimonov had struck at the British from the Victoria Ridge, the Russians would have won the battle.

As it was, the Russian advance, though driving-in the most advanced British positions, was being hampered by the mist which prevented Menshikov and Dannenberg (like Raglan and Canrobert) from forming an accurate assessment of the situation and issuing the appropriate orders. Also, the fighting began to break up into a series of bitter, isolated encounters, shrouded by fog, and separated one from another by trees and brushwood. Men were killed by unseen enemies firing indiscriminately through the mist, or stumbled without warning onto knots of their foes. Many soldiers were shot down as they marched through the swirling vapour to get to grips with their invisible opponents.

The British troops had to cope not merely with a surprise attack but also with damp cartridges and caps, for during the wet night rain had seeped down the barrels of many of the stacked rifles and muskets. Captain Elton of the 2nd Battalion of the Border Regiment (the 55th) discovered to his horror 'that only about fifteen muskets out of the company would go off and out of those fifteen only six men would follow him.' But:

> there was nothing to be done but push to the front and I soon joined the advanced picket which I found in much the same state with regard to the arms as my own. We retired gradually before them as they were coming on in masses of columns supported with a very powerful artillery, and soon had more desperate work almost hand to hand in thick brushwood with the guns playing on us in a most fearful way, and ours answering them over our heads, while we were firing musketry into each other at fifteen and twenty paces distant, now and then charging and driving them back with the bayonet and then being driven back by superior numbers again.

The Russian guns meanwhile had been hauled up to Shell Hill, and began firing accurately into the camp of the 2nd Division on Home Ridge. Some time after 7 am General Bosquet, whose troops on the Sapouné Ridge were under fire from Gorchakov's men from the south-east, hurried to the British positions with offers of assistance. Sir George Cathcart, the commander of the 4th Division, and Sir George Brown, of the Light Division, declined Bosquet's offer; Cathcart (politely) because he considered his men were doing well, Brown (more brusquely) as if offended by the notion of needing the French to bail out his men. Fortunately Bosquet decided, after the Duke of Cambridge (of the 1st Division) had also indicated that he needed no support, to keep his regiments ready to move towards either Inkerman or Balaclava as necessary.

The battle had now developed into a series of spontaneous encounters, quite impossible to direct or coordinate. In this sense Inkerman hardly deserves the description of 'battle' at all, except as the 'soldiers' battle'. One of the main reasons, apart from the mist, for the peculiar character of the engagement lay in the activities of Brigadier-General Pennefather, effectively in command of the 2nd Division. Pennefather early on decided to 'feed the pickets', that is, to send reinforcements to his hard-pressed divisional outposts. This decision contributed a great deal to the break-up of the solid Russian advance into a number of scattered encounters.

Brigadier-General Pennefather and Staff (Fenton).

Nonetheless the Russians continued to make progress. Their artillery relentlessly pounded the British positions from Shell Hill; Soimonov and Paulov's columns were edging closer and closer to each other; and by sheer weight of numbers the Russians were pushing their enemies back.

The British troops fought heroically to maintain their positions. The men of the Light Division, firing their Miniés with devastating accuracy, did terrible execution among the Tomsk, Koliwan and Katerinburg regiments. The men of the 77th Regiment pushed back a mass of Russians, kicking, punching, stabbing and clubbing them into retreat; 183 men of the 49th, led by Colonel Bellairs, repulsed a whole battalion of the enemy; Colonel Mauleverer, with two hundred troops of the 2nd Division, headed a ferocious bayonet charge against four battalions of the Borodino Regiment. Everywhere British units (most of which had not even breakfasted), bayonets wet with blood, flung themselves at their stolid and determined foes with an élan which the French might well have envied.

The numerical superiority of the Russians, however, was beginning to tell. British losses had been heavy, and in many of their advanced positions ammunition was running short. Even though

some of the shattered regiments of Soimonov's force were spilling back across Inkerman Ridge, over Shell Hill poured ten thousand fresh troops intent on breaking the British line.

The hard-pressed 2nd Division were fighting desperately round the Kitspur and the Sandbag Battery, to the north-east of Home Ridge. Here the Russians were repeatedly driven back by rifle butts and bayonets as they swarmed forward over the churned-up ground slippery with mud and drenched in blood. But at last the determined grey-coated enemy drove the men of the 2nd Division off the Kitspur.

Rallying round the Colours, by Seccombe.

Then, dramatically looming out of the mist, and with superb timing, a line of towering Grenadiers advanced on the Kitspur. The Guards Brigade had in fact been tramping for some time towards the centre of the battle from their camp a mile to the rear. Now they flung themselves into the bloody struggle on the Kitspur. Within minutes their immaculate formation was lost (much to the chagrin of the divisional commander, the Duke of Cambridge), and the Guards, together with the nearby Line Regiments, became part of the tumultuous melée around the Kitspur and the Sandbag Battery.

Sir George Cathcart, meanwhile, had sent one of his brigades along the slope to the right of the Guards. Unfortunately the Russians needed countering on the left, and Cathcart's men were soon under fire from that direction. The commander of the 4th Division remarked, accurately enough, 'I fear we are in a mess. We must try the bayonet.' Almost immediately afterwards he was killed by a musket-ball.

The Russians were now gaining the upper hand on the Kitspur; the Guards began to retreat, and the Duke of Cambridge had his horse shot from under him. The situation was saved for the time being by the unheralded appearance of a regiment of French infantry who dashed the Russians back once more.

It was now about 9 am. The rain eased off, and the mist began to break up. It was evident that the main Russian attack was now developing on the Home Ridge where General Dannenberg led six thousand troops in echelon formation. Against this menace the allies could muster only three thousand men. A Russian victory now seemed the most likely outcome, for Dannenberg had a large reserve, and General Gorchakov had his twenty-two thousand men near the Sapouné Heights.

The Russian guns now began to drop their shells and roundshot among Lord Raglan's staff. Raglan himself remained as cool and collected as ever, and, when an ADC begged him to move further off, replied, 'Yes, they do seem to be firing at us a little, but I think I get a better view here than in most places.' Shortly afterwards, however, a shell penetrated the body of Colonel Somerset's horse and blew the unfortunate creature into fragments of bone and entrail, though not injuring the rider. Almost simultaneously General Strangways, who had served with Raglan at Waterloo, had his leg taken off by a roundshot. As polite and calm as his Commander-in-Chief, Strangways said, 'Will someone be kind enough to lift me off my horse?' Within two hours he was dead.

 The battle now reached its height. The 2nd and 4th Divisions, and the Guards, were beginning to tire, and there were no British reinforcements to send in. General Pennefather rode among his men, roaring them on to greater efforts. But British losses had been heavy. Moreover, not only was Dannenberg pressing on, but fresh columns of Russian infantry could be seen marching along the Quarry Ravine towards the road block known as The Barrier.

At last, between 10 and 11 am, Lord Raglan decided to call on the French for immediate support. 'Ah!' said the relieved and delighted General Bosquet, 'I knew it.' The morale of the struggling

The Charge of the Guards at Inkerman.

British troops around the Kitspur was lifted sky-high by the arrival of the French, their bugles shrilling '*Père Casquette*'. Three battalions of Zouaves and Algerians came in at a run, bugles blowing and drums rat-tat-tatting, while Bosquet shouted in Arabic, 'Prove yourselves, children of fire!'

As the French poured in to support their British allies, the tide of the battle slowly turned against the Russians. At the Kitspur, Coldstreams, Algerians and Zouaves charged the enemy and drove them down the hill, bayoneting a good many of them in the process. 'They are panthers,' exclaimed Bosquet approvingly. 'They are panthers bounding into the bush.'

While the Russians were being thus assailed by bounding French panthers and stoical British bulldogs, two 18-pounder guns had been dragged on to Home Ridge. Their fire was directed against the Russian batteries situated on Shell Hill from where the enemy had been pouring a deadly cannonade into the British positions. Colonel Dickson's gunners quickly found the range of Shell Hill, and within minutes the two heavy guns were systematically smashing the Russian batteries to pieces. As the Russian guns faltered, the French also got their heavy artillery into action, and soon twelve of their guns were completing the rout of the Russian batteries on Shell Hill aided by an heroic infantry assault by an assorted force from the Light and the 4th Divisions.

Between midday and 1 o'clock, General Dannenberg, without consulting his superior officer Prince Menshikov, decided to give up the battle and leave the allies in possession of Inkerman Ridge. Though there was a rough numerical parity (about fourteen thousand on each side) between the allied and Russian troops locked together in the battle area, the Russians had suffered appalling losses. The Borodino and Tarutin Regiments had earlier left the field; the 1st Brigade of the Selinghinsk Regiment had been routed and driven back to the Chernaya. But more crippling had been the terrible slaughter of Russian officers in Soimonov's 10th Division and Paulov's 11th Division. Despite their heavy losses the Russians managed to effect an orderly withdrawal, covered by the Vladimir Regiment.

Admittedly the Russian withdrawal was made easier by the allied failure to follow up their success. Canrobert, who had been wounded in the arm by a shell splinter, refused to pursue the enemy when he learned of the depleted state of the British battalions, though he warmly applauded General Pennefather's conviction that, if reinforced, he (Pennefather) 'could lick them to the very Devil!'

As it happened, the Russians had been licked severely enough. Of their attacking force of some forty thousand, they lost 10,729 men, killed, wounded or prisoners (including six generals and 256 officers). The British lost 597 killed and 1,860 wounded, out of which 39 officers were killed and 91 wounded. The French lost 130 killed and 750 wounded, with 13 officers killed and 91 wounded.

Three days after the battle, burial parties were still busy at work. At least four thousand Russian corpses were shovelled into communal graves, and wounded enemy soldiers were continually being

British surgical instruments, including a saw for amputating limbs.

discovered amid the brushwood where their terrible screams caused a troubled General Pennefather to move out of earshot. The allied corpses (of which the overwhelming majority were British) were often frozen in the violent postures characteristic of hand-to-hand fighting. Moreover, to judge from the expressions of terror and hatred on many of the faces a considerable number of the wounded had (as at the Alma) been bayoneted to death by the Russians. When a formal complaint against these barbarities was delivered to Prince Menshikov he replied that certain cases were undoubtedly due to the 'outraged piety of an eminently religious people ... who had been filled with horror' on learning that French troops had pillaged a Russian church near Quarantine Bay.

For many of the wounded there was the usual short shrift of the surgeon's knife. Round the ill-equipped medical tents that served as operating theatres, amputated limbs were piled in neat heaps. Chloroform was 'but seldom used because it occupied so much time'. Also it was considered that the 'smart use of the knife is a powerful stimulant, and it is much better to hear a man bawl lustily than to see him sink silently into the grave'. After field surgery the wounded were shipped off to Scutari, many perishing either at sea or in the squalid hospital wards.

It was by no means clear in the immediate aftermath of Inkerman whether the British sacrifices had been worthwhile. Though both London and Paris claimed a glorious victory, and Raglan was promoted to Field-Marshal and Bosquet to the Legion of Honour, the allied governments soon took a more sober view of the situation. True, the Russian offensive had been broken at Inkerman, but at a high cost. The British expeditionary force had lost too many of its hardened and experienced officers and men; maybe a high proportion of its most courageous troops had also fallen at the Alma, Balaclava and Inkerman. The magnificent spirit that had characterised the redcoated regiments from the landing at Calamita to Inkerman was never to be fully recaptured in the subsequent campaign.

Sebastopol, moreover, still stood. Indeed the Russian citadel seemed positively to thrive under siege conditions, and the allies postponed any idea of a direct assault. As for the Russian army, it had proved itself to be a formidable and durable, if heavy-footed, fighting force; it could, furthermore, be reinforced from inland. The allied armies had acquitted themselves satisfactorily: the British with their splendid opportunist resistance, the French with their well-timed intervention at the crucial point of the battle. But at divisional and company level the encounter had revealed the frightening inadequacies of field communications; the field telephone had not yet been invented and amid the crash of rifle fire and the shifting mists of Inkerman, verbal orders and bugle calls often went unnoticed, or misinterpreted. It was expecting too much to hope that individual courage would continue to compensate for chaotic communications and ill-informed strategic appraisals.

As winter closed in round the huddled armies, General Buller of the 4th Division complained that 'everything present and future is most damnable, that the Anglo-French army is in a very nasty position, and that nothing can be more dismal for the future'. And further, and more comfortably, afield, the Earl of Clarendon, the British Foreign Secretary, wrote to the British ambassador in Paris that the dubious victory of Inkerman had promoted despair and apprehension, and that the army might well be unable to sustain another such 'triumph'.

Chapter 7

Administrative Confusion

The day after Inkerman the allied artillery bombarded Sebastopol, while a British council of war met to decide whether the assault on the town planned earlier should now take place. An astounding variety of views were put forward: from an immediate attack while the Russians were demoralised after their rebuff at Inkerman, to the evacuation of the Crimea altogether. To this last proposal, Lord Raglan pointed out that the army could not pull out and leave its French and Turkish allies in the lurch. It was finally decided to provide winters quarters on the heights above Sebastopol, and to await the arrival of reinforcements.

Properly provided for, the army could have taken the coming winter in its stride. But it was not properly provided for. An incredible administrative chaos was to be made even more unbearable by one of the worst Crimean winters in living memory. To be fair, Lord Raglan was well aware of the administrative shortcomings of his subordinates, and he worked hard to avert some of the threats to the army's comfort and welfare. In particular, Raglan had known, even before the Battle of Balaclava, that the Crimean winter, though frequently mild, could be appallingly severe. He had even told the Secretary of State for War, the Duke of Newcastle, of this possibility, but the Duke had pooh-poohed the notion and had sent, by way of reply, a book that claimed that the Crimean winter was 'one of the mildest and finest in the world'.

On 14 November, as if to presage the sufferings that were about to envelop the army, a terrible storm broke after five days of torrential downpour. Balaclava harbour was lashed by violent winds, and huge waves crashed against the cliff faces. Outside the comparative shelter of the harbour conditions were much worse, and a good many ships were forced to ride out the storm in a deep and dangerous anchorage nearby. Tragically there was plenty of room in Balaclava harbour, but the port authorities obstinately denied the ships outside entry – though a few desperate captains forced their way into the narrow waters.

Opposite Before Sebastopol, November 1854.

The losses sustained by the British ships were catastrophic. Of the vessels in or near Balaclava harbour twenty-one were smashed to pieces on the rocks, and eight badly damaged. Five transport ships were sunk off Eupatoria, and a considerable number near Katcha Bay. Among the ships lost was the *Prince*, a fine steamship, which went to the bottom with her full cargo including forty thousand pairs of boots; the modern French warship *Henri IV* was also lost, and on board the *Retribution* which, though she lost two anchors, did not sink, the indisposed Duke of Cambridge (according to Cornet Fisher) was 'most undignified, and held the Steward's hand, bewailing his fate, saying "Oh! Is it come to this? Oh! Oh! We shall be lost." '

On land too the storm caused great havoc, though naturally without the loss of life incurred at sea. Army tents were blown to shreds, and hospital marquees ripped apart. Tables and chairs were whirled away, and the 4th Regiment saw its big ceremonial drum blow across to the Russian lines. Part of the roof of the farm house that lodged Lord Raglan was torn off; trees were uprooted, barrels hurled around like cricket balls, and heavy wagons blown along dragging their oxen with them like 'mere kittens'. Men crouched behind walls for shelter, or lay in muddy, freezing holes in the ground. Many of the sick and wounded were left drenched and helpless as the hospital tents were whisked away like bits of paper.

At about 2 o'clock in the afternoon the wind abated, but snow began to fall, covering the muddy roads with a treacherous surface. The cold, wet and hungry men began to collect their equipment together, and tried to salvage what they could from the tangled, mud-stained debris that surrounded them. Loose horses were everywhere. Balaclava harbour and the nearby coast line were clogged with ruined equipment and supplies: planks, spars, tons of gunpowder, hundreds of thousands of cartridges, woollen stockings, boots, surgical supplies, coats and flannel drawers.

To cap it all, some of the sodden British troops were issued with green coffee – doubtless to put new heart into them. The commanding officer of the 1st Foot wrote bitterly that:

> A ration of green raw coffee berry was served out, a mockery in the midst of all this misery. Nothing to roast coffee in, nothing to grind it, no fire, no sugar; and unless it was meant that we eat it as horses do barley, I don't see what use the men could make of it, except that they have just done, pitched it into the mud! How patient those men of mine; how admirably they behave. In silence they bear with all privations; away they go ... ankle deep in mud, and wet to the skin, down to the trenches.

The British common soldier was soon to have his character and stoical forbearance put to the harshest test. The day before the great storm, Filder, the Commissary-General, had written gloomily to the British Treasury:

> I am full of apprehension as to our power of keeping this Army supplied during the coming winter ... In this crowded little harbour only a proportion of our vessels can be admitted at a time ... With all the siege and other stores which are being disembarked, we can do little more

than land sufficient supplies to keep pace with the daily consumption of the troops; and to add to our difficulties, the road from the harbour to the camp, not being a made one, is impassable after heavy rains; our obstacles in these respects will increase as the winter comes. We shall have many more stores to convey than we have hitherto had – fuel, for instance. In short, I am full of anxiety and dread on the subject.

After the storm there were anxious attempts to blame the increasingly embarrassing and unforgivable inadequacies in supply upon the ravages of the unexpected tempest. The allegedly impassable roads were also cited, but there is evidence that the difficulties in this respect were exaggerated by contemporaries since the road over the Col continued usable.

The plain fact was that in Balaclava there was no lack of food, clothing or stores. The problem lay in moving the supplies up to the heights above. This proved to be a task beyond the Commis-

The great storm of November 1854.

Crimean winter.
Balaclava in the snow.

sariat, not because of the freezing muddy tracks, but because there was not enough forage to feed the pack animals (which in turn prevented more transport animals being brought to help the situation). So serious was the forage shortage, in fact, that the cavalry horses were literally starving throughout November, and reduced to eating each others' tails and manes; on 1 December Lord Lucan informed Lord Raglan that the Cavalry Division had practically ceased to exist. Half-starved pack animals stumbled on their twelve-hour-long trek from Balaclava to the encampments, and back. Though a labour force of Turks was brought in (too late as it happened) to improve the roads, they found the earth too hard to dig, and were soon dying in such numbers that a large amount of time was spent in burying them. Not until the construction of the Balaclava railway line in January 1855 by British navvies, was it possible to move anything like enough supplies up to the heights above the town.

Balaclava, as the winter gripped the Crimea, was a place of nightmarish chaos. Much of the blame for this rested with Admiral Boxer, who was in charge of transport arrangements at Constantinople. Due to his inefficiency, ships arrived at Balaclava without notice and with nobody sure what supplies they carried. Some ships sailed into Constantinople and were promptly sent back again unloaded. Boxer seemed to have no clear idea as to how many ships were at his disposal, and often claimed that no transport was available while empty ships were lying at his docks. His office was a place of indescribable chaos, and he appeared to keep no records. Lord Raglan wrote despairingly, 'As regards Admiral Boxer, I am powerless. No man can make him a man of arrangements.'

On the quayside at Balaclava there was unbelievable confusion. Flour poured out of split sacks in great damp lumps; ammunition boxes, tent pegs, broken pieces of wood, rotting meat and powder barrels lay jumbled together; bales of urgently needed clothing were used as stepping-stones through the mud and filth; rats and dogs scavenged; Turkish soldiers died like flies in the makeshift hospitals – mostly commandeered hovels. In the waters of the harbour floated a hideous refuse: bloated corpses, amputated limbs, dead horses, mules, cats and dogs, rotting sheep's carcasses, human excrement, smashed packing cases and waterlogged bales of hay. The stench everywhere was appalling.

The problems were due not merely to the climate, to the storm, to clogged roads or to the stupidity and incompetence of individuals – though these were all potent factors. Over and above difficulties of this nature was the grotesque lack of coordination between the different administrative branches of the army. The following staffs of officials were responsible for the army's supply, welfare, and equipment: the Secretary-of-State for War and the Colonies, theoretically responsible for military policy, but to a large measure occupied in Colonial Office business; the Secretary-at-War, dealing with army finance and business; the Commander-in-Chief, who was unable to initiate any measure involving finance without the agreement of the Secretary-at-War; the Adjutant-General, who dealt with recruiting, discipline, pay, arms and clothing; the Quartermaster-General, who was responsible for movement, quartering, barracks, camps and transport – though no transport corps existed; the Board of General Officers, who advised the Adjutant-General on clothing and equipment; the Master-General of the Ordnance (a post once filled by Lord Raglan), the commander of the artillery and engineers, and the head of the Board of Ordnance; the commanding officers of regiments, who dealt with contractors for fuel and rations; the Commissariat officers who, while the army was overseas, provided rations and fuel, managed butcheries and bakeries, and were responsible to the Treasury; the Medical Staff Corps composed of doctors and purveyors (who were quartermasters to the hospitals), who were responsible for various matters to the Secretary-at-War, the Commander-in-Chief and the Ordnance Office; the Paymaster-General who was cashier for the army treasury.

The duties of these various officials were ill-defined. There was no coordination, and little effort to adapt to changing circumstances – not even those of war. Under the sustained and bitter

criticism that the war provoked, some adaptation was made to this administrative machine. In March 1855 a Land Transport Corps was formed, and in June 1855 a new Medical Corps was set up to provide hospital services. Other reforms dribbled through after the war was over.

At the outset of the war, however, the administrators, and many of the officers, worried little over the common soldiers' conditions. Indeed, it was even feared that too much pampering would spoil

Commissariat Difficulties, by William Simpson.

the iron resistance of the rank and file. Men who had lived through the famine years of the hungry 1840s, it was argued, would be slow to complain even of quarter-rations. This attitude was rendered all the more unforgivable by the careless luxury displayed by certain officers: Lord Cardigan dined and slept aboard his yacht; Colonel Darby Griffiths of the Scots Greys came to the Crimea with a French chef and provisions supplied by Fortnum and Mason; Lord Rokeby, who arrived in February 1855 to take over the Guards Brigade from Lord Bentinck, brought a patent water closet (which the Zouaves soon stole for boiling soup in); some wives were shipped out, and the newly-married Lord George Paget actually received Lord Raglan's permission to retire with his bride during the winter of 1854–5.

Despite the care and hard work of countless devoted officers, despite the unceasing toil of Lord Raglan, General Airey and others, morale deteriorated sharply. Lord Raglan's extraordinary refusal to show himself to his men, and his conviction that secretive visits to the encampments, mostly under the cover of night, served the best purpose, led to the widespread belief that he cared nothing for the troops' welfare. One young officer was talking one day to a brother officer who confessed that he had no idea of what Lord Raglan looked like:

> 'I never saw him,' said the officer. So I said to him, 'Well, there he is, going into the hospital.' 'What,' said the officer, '*that* Lord Raglan? Why, I have seen him constantly, but I never dreamed that was Lord Raglan.' The fact was Lord Raglan walked or rode about with perhaps no one with him or perhaps one ADC and those who did not know him personally never guessed, and if told would not often believe, that *that* unattended man was their commander.

By the end of November the plight of the army had stirred *The Times* to move into the attack against the administrative incompetence and muddle in the Crimea. William Russell, the newspaper's principal war correspondent, had been asking awkward questions and revealing embarrassing truths from the outset of the campaign. Though many of the junior officers, who supplied him with first-hand information, enjoyed his company, others, particularly the high-ranking officers, came to dislike him intensely. Captain Clifford described Russell plainly but not inaccurately when he wrote:

> He is a vulgar low Irishman, an Apostate Catholic (but that is neither here nor there), but he has the gift of the gab, uses his pen as well as his tongue, sings a good song, drinks anyone's brandy and water, and smokes as many cigars as foolish young officers will let him, and he is

'MIS(S) MANAGEMENT' A wry comment on the failings of the British supplies to the men at the front.

> looked upon by most in camp as a Jolly Good Fellow. He is just the sort of chap to get information, particularly out of youngsters. And I assure you, more than one 'Nob' has thought best to give him a shake of the hand rather than a cold shoulder *en passant*, for [he] is rather an awkward gentleman to be on bad terms with.

Lord Raglan and his staff chose to give Russell the cold shoulder. For his part, Russell openly displayed his dislike of Raglan and most of the generals. His editor in London, John Delane, decided on 25 November to sanction a journalistic attack on Lord Raglan and his staff, and on that day *The Times*' dispatch from Russell began the indictment:

> It is now pouring rain – the skies are black as ink – the wind is howling over the staggering tents – the trenches are turned into dykes – in the tents the water is sometimes a foot deep – our men have not either warm or waterproof clothing – they are out for twelve hours at a time in the trenches – they are plunged into the inevitable miseries of a winter campaign – and not a soul seems to care for their comfort or even for their lives.

There was admittedly a lot to attack. Russell pointed out the difficult conditions under which the army lived and fought:

> The oldest soldiers never witnessed or heard of a campaign in which general officers were obliged to live out in tents on the open field, for the want of a roof to cover them, and generals who passed their youth in the Peninsula War, and who had witnessed a good deal of fighting since that time in various parts of the world, were unanimous in declaring that they never knew or read of a war in which officers were exposed to such hardships. They landed without anything but what they could carry, and they marched beside their men, slept by them, fought by them, and died by them, undistinguished from them in any respect, except by the deadly epaulet and swordbelt, which have cost so many lives to this country. The survivors were often unable to get their things from on board ship. They laid down at night in the clothes which they wore during the day; many delicately nurtured youths never changed shirt and shoes for weeks together, and they were deprived of the use of water for ablution, except to a very limited extent.

There was much worse to come, even for less delicately nurtured youths, as the battles developed and when winter struck. Men took all sorts of rough and ready devices to keep out the cold. Some put:

long stockings outside their rags or trousers; some had garters made from old knapsacks; others had leggings made from sheepskins, bullocks' hides, horse hides – anything to keep out the extreme cold ... Our men's coats were nothing but rags tacked together. As for head dress some had mess tin covers that could be pulled down well over the ears; others had coverings for the head made out of old blankets four or five times doubled ... Some of their beards and moustaches were almost two inches long, and sometimes these were so frozen that they could not open their mouths until they could get a fire to thaw them.

The notorious Barrack Hospital at Scutari, where Florence Nightingale won immortality, by Lady Alicia Blackwood.

But the worst horrors were reserved for the wounded, or those suffering from disease. Quite early on in the campaign it was evident that hospital conditions were appallingly inadequate. At the hospital at Balaclava nurse Elizabeth Davis recalled:

I began to open some of their wounds. The first that I touched was a case of frost bite. The toes of both the man's feet fell off with the bandages.

The hand of another fell off at the wrist. It was a fortnight, or from that to six weeks, since the wounds of many had been looked at and dressed ... One soldier had been wounded at Alma ... His wound had not been dressed for five weeks, and I took at least a quart of maggots from it. From many of the other patients I removed them in handfuls.

Some of the sick and wounded must be accounted lucky even to have got as far as a filthy, verminous and overcrowded hospital. At Balaclava, Mrs Duberly, the wife of an officer of the 8th Hussars, recorded her impressions in her journal:

> I hear the sick are dying at an average of eighty per diem. With some horror (not much) and a great deal of curiosity, I watched from over the taffrail of the Star of the South the embarkation of some Russian prisoners and English soldiers (all wounded) for Scutari. The dignified indifference of the medical officer, who stood with hands in his pockets, gossiping in the hospital doorway – the rough, indecent way in which the poor howling wretches were hauled along the quay, and bundled, some with one, and others with both legs amputated, into the bottom of the boat, without a symptom of a stretcher or bed, was truly an edifying exemplification of the golden rule 'Do to others as you would be done by'.

Soon letters were reaching horrified relatives in Britain, as when Captain Godman of the 5th Dragoon Guards wrote of the shipment of wounded to the hospital at Scutari:

> I believe you think in England that every preparation has been taken to make the sick and wounded as comfortable as possible. Such is not the case. Indeed anything so disgraceful as the whole department it is impossible to imagine. The other day I was told on good authority that five hundred men went to Scutari after Alma, sick and wounded in one ship, and attended by two surgeons and five men, one of whom died on the way, and the poor fellows had no one to assist them or look after them. On their arrival no preparations for their reception had been made. There are twelve hundred wounded at Scutari, and four thousand in hospital altogether there. I heard from one hospital sergeant who went on board one of the ships at Balaclava the other day that the state of things there is just as bad or worse, the ship crowded with men shouting for water, and no one to attend them.

Opposite Florence Nightingale.

It was at Scutari that Florence Nightingale battled as valiantly as any soldier in the field to improve conditions so vile as to beggar description. The men were piled up in corridors, lying on unscrubbed, rotting floors crawling with vermin. In the wards there were at first no screens behind which the doctors could carry out the brisk and grisly business of amputation which was almost the only kind of surgery performed. In Florence Nightingale's early days in the hospital at Scutari there were more than a thousand patients suffering from acute diarrhoea and only twenty chamber pots to go round! The privies were blocked up and an inch of liquid filth floated over the floor. Furthermore, 'The majority of the cases at the Barrack Hospital were suffering from diarrhoea, they had no slippers and no shoes, and they had to go into this

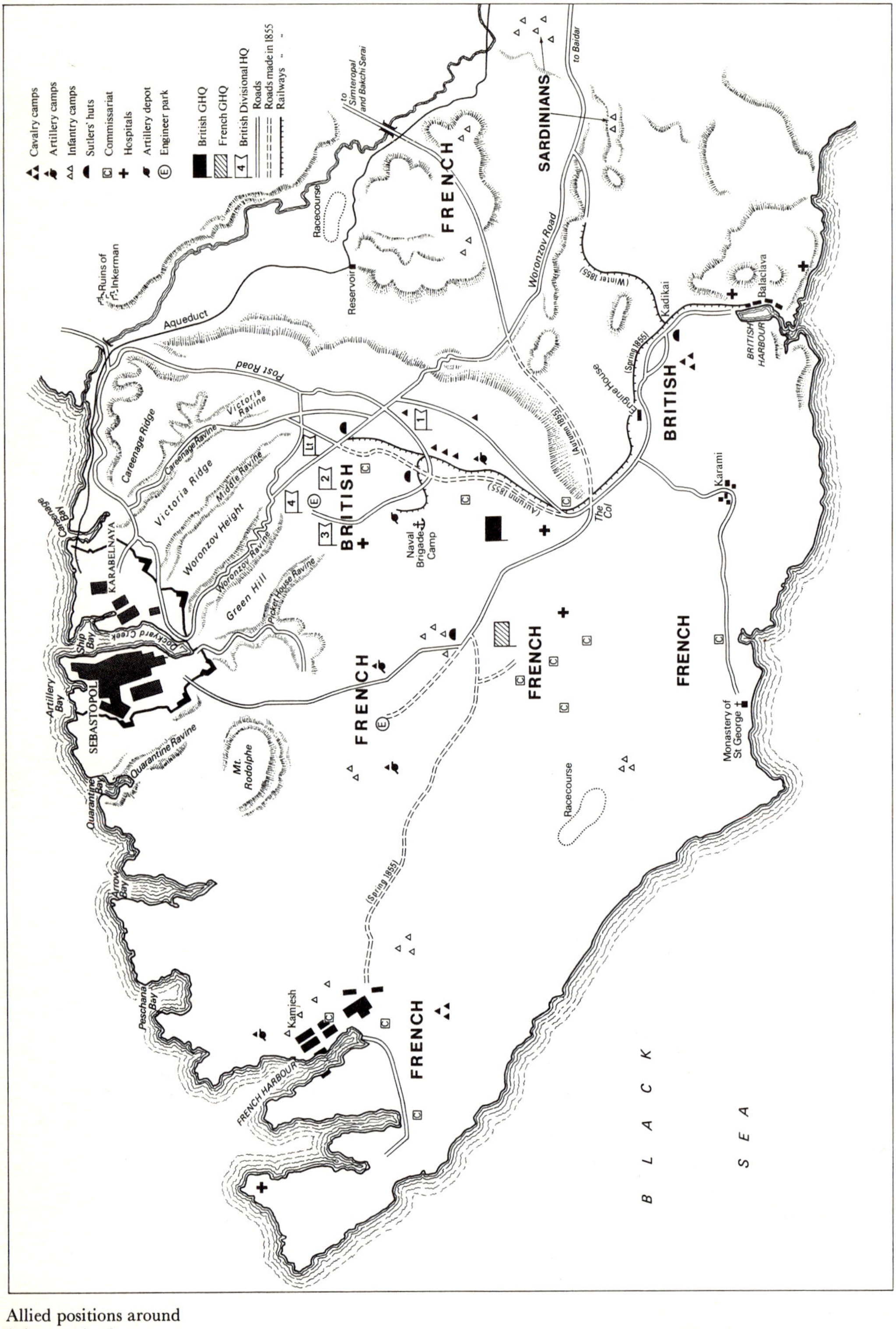

Allied positions around Sebastopol, 1855.

filth so that gradually they did not trouble to go into the lavatory chamber itself.' The men's food often lay in this revolting mess. It was small wonder that Florence Nightingale wrote despairingly, 'We have erysipelas, fever and gangrene ... the dysentery cases have died at the rate of one in two ... the mortality of the operations is frightful... This is only the beginning of things.' The vile stench from the hospital penetrated the walls and could be smelt from some distance away.

Improved conditions in the wards at Scutari.

Florence Nightingale's impact on hospital conditions was remarkable, but not immediate. Indeed, when she first arrived at Scutari on 5 November 1854 with thirty-eight nurses recruited by her in England on the prompting of the Secretary-at-War, the doctors refused her help, and only allowed her nurses to undertake menial duties. But the flood of wounded and sick that poured into the hospitals in the aftermath of Balaclava and Inkerman forced officialdom's hand, and Florence Nightingale's influence grew accordingly. She had a fund of £30,000 to manage, and out of this she purchased some of the necessities so badly needed at the Barrack Hospital. She also worked with incredible energy and devotion, often going without sleep, superintending the multiple tasks that confronted her – cleansing the wards, ensuring that fresh bed linen was available, tending the dying, and arranging for the preparation of special nutritious diets.

Her relentlessly logical mind, and her almost 'masculine' qualities which enabled her to dominate and browbeat those that came into contact with her, made her an irresistible force. An enormous force for good, but in impact less the devotedly feminine 'Lady with the Lamp' than the tough-minded administrative reformer. Dr John Hall, the Inspector General of Hospitals, and Raglan's Principal Medical Officer, immediately recognized her inconvenient strength of character and tried, by a subterfuge, to have her shipped back to Britain. Florence avoided the trap, and she henceforth entertained a deep dislike of Hall, remarking when

he was awarded the KCB that this must stand for 'Knight of the Crimean Burial Grounds'.

Of Florence Nightingale's success in the Crimea there can be no doubt. On her arrival at Scutari the hospital death rate was an appalling 44 per cent; six months' later it had plummeted to 2·2 per cent. She was rewarded with the adulation of the Victorian public, which surrounded her with a sentimental idolisation that stamped her portrait on paper bags and prompted a somewhat mawkish best-selling biography costing one penny. She died in 1910, still held in the highest regard.

The wounded and sick leave Balaclava for Scutari.

The horrors brought so vividly to light by *The Times*, and so vigorously combated by Florence Nightingale and others, shattered the patriotic complacency of opinion at home. The British public was searching furiously for a scapegoat during the winter of 1854–5. Who was to blame? That 'old traitor Aberdeen' (the Prime Minister)? Lord Raglan? His staff? The Secretary of State for War (the Duke of Newcastle)? Queen Victoria put her own misgivings before Lord Raglan in a reasonable but concerned letter written on 1 January 1855:

> The sad privations of the Army, the bad weather and the constant sickness are causes of the deepest concern and anxiety to the Queen and the Prince. The braver her noble Troops are and the more patiently they bear all their trials and sufferings the more miserable we feel at their long continuance.
>
> The Queen trusts that Lord Raglan will be very strict in seeing that no unnecessary privations are incurred by any negligence of those whose duty it is to watch over their wants. The Queen heard that their coffee was given them green instead of its being roasted and several other things of the kind. It has distressed the Queen as she feels so conscious that they should be made as comfortable as circumstances can admit of. The Queen earnestly trusts that the larger amount of warm clothing has not only reached Balaclava but has been distributed and that Lord Raglan has been successful in procuring the means of hutting for the men. Lord Raglan cannot think how much we suffer for the Army and how painfully anxious we are to know that their privations are decreasing.

Lord Raglan replied directly telling the Queen that he could

> with truth assure your Majesty that his whole time and all his thoughts are occupied in endeavouring to provide for the various wants of your Majesty's troops. It has not been in his power to lighten the burden of their duties ... Much having been said, as Lord Raglan has been given to understand, in private letters, of the inefficiency of the staff, he considers it to be due to your Majesty, and a simple act of justice to those individuals, to assure your Majesty that he has every reason to be satisfied with their exertions, their indefatigable zeal, and undeviating close attention to their duties.

On the other hand, Raglan was very much aware of deficiencies in medical care and supply. In December 1854 he issued a General Order that was highly critical of the treatment of the sick and wounded:

> The Commander of the Forces is sorry to have to animadvert very strongly upon the conduct of the medical department, in an instance which came under his observation yesterday. The sick went down from the camp to Balaclava under the charge of a medical officer of the division to which they respectively belonged; but on their arrival there it was found that no preparations had been made for their reception.

> The Commander of the Forces is aware that Deputy Inspector-General of Hospitals Doctor Dumbreck gave the necessary order verbally to the staff medical officer at Balaclava, but that officer neglected to inform his superior and the consequence was that the sick, many of them in a very suffering state, remained in the streets for several hours, exposed to the very inclement weather. The name of the officer who was guilty of this gross neglect is known to the Commander of the Forces. He will not now publish it, but he warns him to be careful in future, and to be cautious how he again exposes himself to censure. Doctor Dumbreck will, in future, give his orders in writing, addressed to the responsible officer. When a convoy of sick is sent from the camp either to the hospitals, or to be placed on board ship, it is henceforth to be accompanied not only by a medical officer, but likewise by the DAQMG of the Division, who will precede it to the place of deposit, and take such steps as may ensure the due reception and care of the men confided to his charge.

But Lord Raglan's censorious interventions could not halt the flood of private and public criticism. Towards the end of December 1854 a *Times* leader thundered:

> There are people who think it a less happy consummation of affairs that the Commander-in-Chief and his staff should survive alone on the heights of Sebastopol, decorated, ennobled, duly named in despatch after despatch, and ready to return home to enjoy pensions and honours amid the bones of fifty thousand British soldiers, than that the equanimity of office and the good-humour of society should be disturbed by a single recall or a new appointment over the heads now in command.

Lieutenant-Colonel Anthony Sterling, who served in the Crimea, later published *The Story of the Highland Brigade in the Crimea*, in which he expressed a variety of hard-hitting judgements on the conduct of the war. He attacked the 'gossip' of British journalists in the Crimea and also the rapid promotion vouchsafed to the aristocratic officers of the élitist Guards Regiments. But he also had more general and more telling criticisms:

> The mistake that has been made has been a very common one in our country, viz, not keeping up certain military establishments in peace, because people took it into their heads that war would never come. In France there is a permanent waggon-train always organised, a permanent commissariat, and also a permanent ambulance; these three departments hang very much upon one another. The English people having destroyed these above-named departments, which existed during the Spanish War, or which rather were then formed, its Government, on deciding upon war, should have instantly begun to organize them again. This is a matter of time as well as money; there has now been time enough allowed to slip away; but nothing is really organized yet.
>
> And this when our army belongs, not only to the richest country in

The Balaclava railway.

> the world, but to the country richest in horses and ships. Many of the Staff and general officers were appointed from interest. It seemed either that Lord Raglan did not expect war, he intended to do all the work himself ... Estcourt was pitch-forked into the important office of adjutant-general, with high pay and powers; but his business is discipline, which he endeavours to combine with amiability; a most charming man in private life, but quite out of place here.

The huge volume of criticism and complaint had its effect. In February 1855 the Aberdeen government fell; the bellicose Lord Palmerston became Prime Minister and Lord Panmure went to the War Office. The new administration was apparently determined to make drastic improvements in the running of the war and to overhaul the management of military affairs as a whole. This resulted in some improvement in the organisation and administration of the British army. The French, on the other hand, who had not suffered such acute catastrophes of supply and organisation as the British, did not carry out equivalent reforms.

As spring approached, the administrative chaos in the Crimea was slowly cleared. Provisions were located in separate depots on the plateau above Balaclava; the railway line was completed, and now reached the Woronzov Road; more Turkish labour was recruited to carry out improvements; transport was borrowed from the French, and boatloads of Spanish mules arrived. The confusion in Balaclava itself was tackled with determination, and soon supplies were being sent with comparatively little delay to the troops, while the cheating contractors and sutlers were purged.

By March 1855, the morale of the depleted British army had been largely restored; the soldiers' bellies were filled with the fresh meat and fruit shipped in to Balaclava, and sporting activities (including cricket) were being organised.

As the army shook off the frozen grip of winter, and stirred itself from its lethargy and despair, it was ready once more to attempt the capture of Sebastopol.

Chapter 8

The Siege of Sebastopol

The allied siege of Sebastopol barely deserves the description of 'siege'. Having failed to attack the town at earlier, more propitious, opportunities, and then virtually ceasing their operations in order to contend with the winter, the allied armies had little option, with the advent of spring, but to take the defences of Sebastopol bit by bit. There were enormous problems in such tactics. To begin with, Sebastopol was not encircled by allied troops; the northern and eastern approaches to the town were wide open, and Russian forces could march in and out as they wished; supplies could also be brought in to sustain the garrison.

Nor were the defenders of Sebastopol a numerically inferior force subjected to the morale-sapping anxieties of dwindling rations and military isolation. Indeed it was the besiegers who had to look to means of boosting their numbers. By the beginning of February 1855 the strength of the British army had declined alarmingly: there were about eleven thousand fit men, and twenty-three thousand sick and wounded. The French, on the other hand, had ninety thousand men, and with further reinforcements arriving, they were becoming decidedly the senior partners in the campaign. Still, it was considered essential to supplement the besieging forces with other units. To achieve this end, twenty thousand Turks with thirty guns arrived at the beginning of April from Omar Pasha's army which was defending Eupatoria. Then there were the foreign mercenaries: nine thousand men of the German Legion, three thousand of the Swiss Legion, and a Polish Legion of 1,500. In May 1855, moreover, fifteen thousand Sardinians arrived, led by De La Marmora. These colourful troops with 'bandit-looking hats with large plumes of black cocks' feathers', at least made a hit among the ladies. The beautiful Lady George Paget thought them 'ravishing', and the gallant De La Marmora arranged for his own private band to play for her morning and night aboard the *Caradoc* in Balaclava harbour.

Opposite The Russians, symbolically led by Prince Michael Dimitri, hurl defiance at the allies before Sebastopol.

Despite these additions to allied numbers, the defences of Sebastopol remained formidable. There was, of course, no continuous defensive stone wall round the town. Except for the round tower of the Malakov and another in the Old Town, there was hardly any stonework in the original defences. Todleben's defences were earthworks reinforced with timber, brushwood and the earth-filled baskets known as gabions. The great earthen rampart that the Russians had thrown up was defended by a palisade of sharpened stakes, then a ditch, beyond which was a rifle pit. On the defensive

The interior of the Malakov, a key defensive position guarding Sebastopol (Fenton).

slope (the glacis), beyond the rifle pit, were other obstacles: abbatis (a tangle of trees and branches); fougasses (holes filled with stones beneath which lay a detonating charge); the ground was also strewn with planks from which projected sharp nails. Beneath the ground, too, the two sides worked to undermine their enemies; elaborate galleries and chambers were dug, and sappers listened intently for evidence of enemy mining, and then struck and destroyed the menacing diggings.

In general, the Russians managed to counter the allied siege operations with comparative ease. Any allied threat was promptly answered (mostly overnight) by Todleben's engineers and sappers.

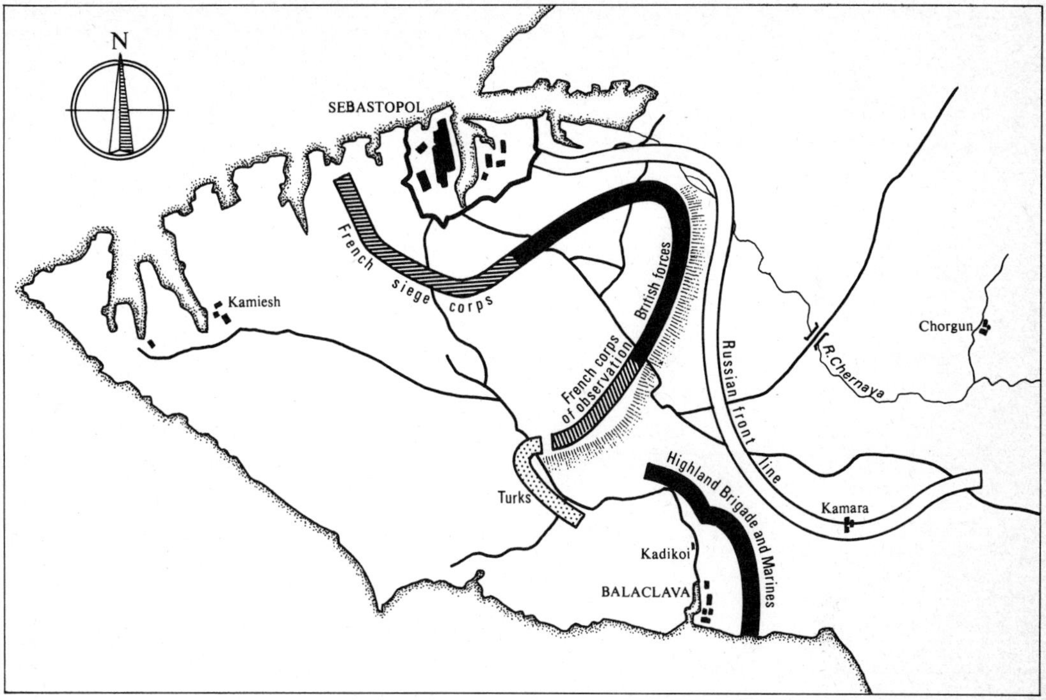

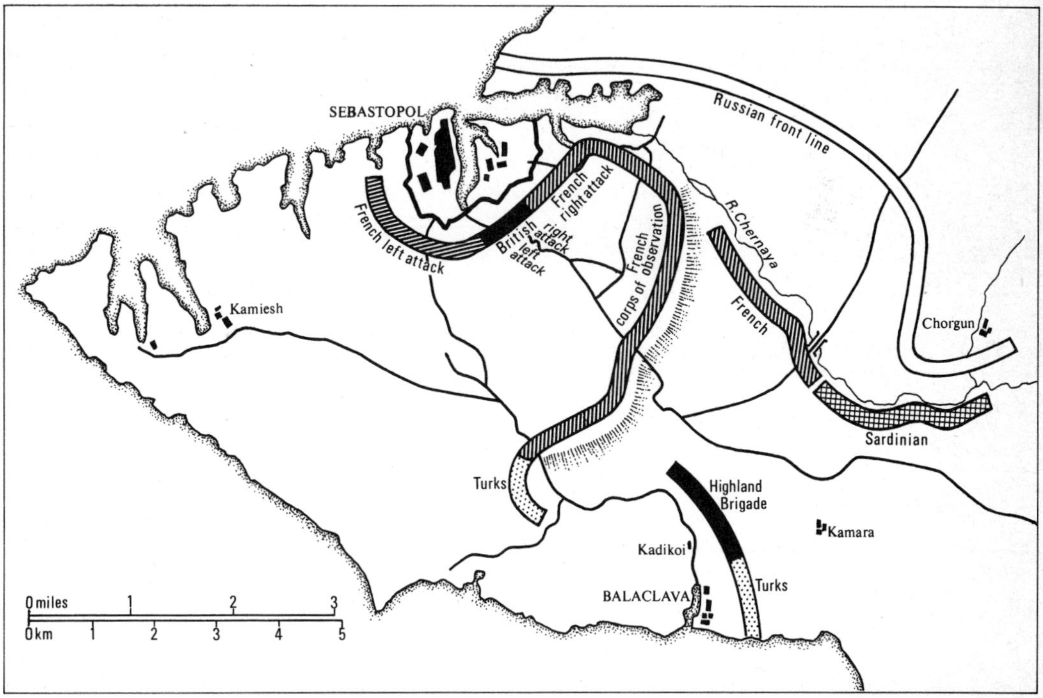

The Allied positions around Sebastopol, (top) in November 1854, (bottom) in May 1855.

Tsar Alexander II, who succeeded to the throne in 1855.

Indeed the besieged (some one hundred thousand troops assisted by ten thousand workmen) were apt to take the initiative against the besiegers; at night raiding parties from the advanced Russian counter-parallels and rifle pits crept up to the allied trenches and attacked their unsuspecting occupants.

The British role in the siege was a modest one, as befitted their now modest numerical contribution. They occupied a small sector in the middle of the siege front, across the Woronzov Road, and facing the Redan and the Greenhill Cemetery. The rest of the army was stretched out on the heights above Balaclava. The French left attack on Sebastopol was directed against the Flagstaff Battery, the Central Bastion and the Quarantine Bastion; the French right

attack was opposite the Malakov, the Little Redan and (by the end of February 1855) the Mamelon.

Repulse of the French from the Little Redan during the Siege of Sebastopol.

The Mamelon, a small hill about four hundred yards in front of the Malakov, was taken by the Russians on the night of 22 February, and quickly converted into a redoubt faced with stone. The capturing of the Mamelon became an urgent priority for the allies, since the British argued that such a success would enable them to attack the Redan, and the French that they would then stand a good chance of taking the Malakov.

On 6 March the allies received a report that the Tsar Nicholas I had died, and had been succeeded by his son Alexander II. Raglan urged Canrobert to strike immediately against the Mamelon since Russian morale might well have been affected by the Tsar's death. Canrobert, however, refused. There were good reasons for the French commander's lack of initiative at this point in the war. On 27 January General Adolphe Niel, the Emperor's aide-de-camp and confidant, had arrived in the Crimea with wide powers of supervision and even control. The Emperor himself was anxious to take as full a part as possible in the campaign – especially since the return of Prince Napoleon ('Plon-Plon') to France in January had left the Imperial army without a Napoleon in the field, and the newly-founded Second Empire needed to keep alive the martial

Heavy guns at the Siege of Sebastopol.

glories associated with the Napoleonic Legend; the Emperor had therefore decided to come to the Crimea and lead his army in the field. While waiting for an appropriate opportunity to descend on the Crimea, Napoleon III badgered Canrobert with instructions and advice. The Emperor had come to the conclusion early in 1855 that Sebastopol would never be taken unless it was properly invested and closed in from all sides. Lord Raglan never accepted this hypothesis, but Canrobert came to accept it, though somewhat grudgingly. At any rate, the French commander remained unwilling to risk a premature assault on Sebastopol.

While the allies vacillated, the Russians, throughout March, pushed their lines forward and continued to build up their defences.

Corporal Philip Smith winning the VC during the assault on the Redan at Sebastopol, by Terence Cuneo.

'Roll Call'. Weary British troops muster in the snow, by Lady Butler.

Interior of the Mamelon.

Lord Raglan, by
Andrew Mortimer.

On 22 March they made a menacing sortie against the French parallels on the Victoria Ridge and were able for a time to establish themselves in the French lines; they then turned against the north flank of the British right attack, but were eventually driven off by artillery fire. It was, to say the least, an embarrassment for the besieging forces, and led to acrimonious exchanges between the British and the French as to how the Russians had been able to open up the French flank.

On 9 April the allies began a second great bombardment of Sebastopol. 520 allied guns (of which only 138 were British) poured 165,000 rounds of ammunition into the town's defences; they were answered by 998 Russian guns, which fired about ninety thousand rounds in reply. For ten days the guns thundered out, resulting in heavy Russian casualties (6,131) mostly among their dangerously exposed infantry units; there were 1,587 French and 263 British casualties.

Unfortunately for the allies the Russian defences were repaired at night through the heroic exertions of Todleben and his men,

Action before Sebastopol, April 1855. A gory Russian version of the siege.

though the Flagstaff Bastion was an exception, being so ruined that the Russians gave it up for lost. But even here, the allies were unable to take advantage of the damage inflicted, even though the French dug themselves up to within a hundred yards of the Flagstaff Bastion. Again Canrobert, harassed by Imperial directives, deferred an assault. Raglan, however, was keen to attack, and a young British subaltern named Charles Gordon, and destined for immortality at Khartoum thirty years later, wrote that the French seemed to be afraid and were 'cramping the movements of the British'. Canrobert did in fact agree to a combined assault on 28 April, but less than twenty-four hours before it was due to take place he called off the operation, arguing that it would be more sensible to await the arrival of twenty thousand French reinforcements and the Imperial Guard.

Relations between the British and French commanders understandably suffered during these inconclusive and abortive events. The British thought that the French were too cautious, the French that the British were awkward junior partners. Though Lord Raglan maintained his habitual cordial relations with senior French officers, others did not, as, for example, when Canrobert opened a Council of War with the rhetorical assertion: 'Gentlemen, we are here for the capture of Sebastopol,' and Admiral Lyons said, quite plainly, 'Oh! That's it, is it?' reducing Admiral Stewart to uncontrollable laughter.

Pressures from outside the Crimea also increased tension, or at least confusion, during March and April 1855. On 15 March a conference opened in Vienna, attended by representatives of Austria, France, Britain, Russia and Turkey, to see if any progress could be made towards a peace. A month later the Emperor Napoleon III touted his plan for a speedy and successful conclusion to the war at a special Council of War at Windsor Castle attended by, among others, Queen Victoria, Prince Albert, the Empress Eugénie, Lord Palmerston, Lord Panmure and Sir John Burgoyne. The Emperor's plan was to divide the forces in the Crimea into four armies: thirty thousand Turks and Egyptians would hold Eupatoria; thirty thousand French and thirty thousand Turks would continue to hold the lines before Sebastopol; a third army, led by Lord Raglan, and composed of twenty-five thousand British, five thousand French, fifteen thousand Sardinians and, hopefully, ten thousand Turks, would drive the Russians off the Mackenzie Heights and advance north towards Simferopol; a fourth army, of seventy thousand French troops, was to go by sea to Alushta on the eastern side of the Crimean peninsula and from there advance towards Simferopol, where it would link up with Raglan's army and proceed to drive the Russians into the sea.

The plan, though vague in some respects, was at least original. Certainly some new coordination of the allied war effort was badly needed, though there was doubt on all sides as to the wisdom of the Emperor's coming to the Crimea to effect such a coordination.

Napoleon III did not, in fact, descend on the Crimea to lead his armies to some latterday Austerlitz (or, more probably, Borodino). He continued, however, to do the next best, or worst, thing, and peppered the unfortunate Canrobert with more instructions. From the end of April, moreover, the Emperor's capacity for interference was rendered doubly potent by the completion of the electric telegraph from Varna to the allied headquarters.

An infuriating demonstration of the efficiency of the electric telegraph followed on 2 May. A combined expedition set sail on that date to Kertch at the entrance of the Sea of Azof. The plan was British in conception and was aimed at cutting off Russian supplies coming from that area, and at opening the Sea of Azof to allied warships which could then attack Russian supply ships coming from the mainland. But two hours after the expeditionary force had set sail a telegram arrived for Canrobert from the Emperor which, though dictated without any knowledge of the Kertch enterprise, tied the French commander's hands by ordering him (among other things) to send all available ships to Constantinople, and forbidding him to divert any troops from the reduction of Sebastopol.

Canrobert wrestled with his conscience, and then decided to recall the French component in the Kertch force. The French Admiral Bruat could not be persuaded by the British to turn a blind eye, like Nelson, to the order. The French came back, and the British had no option but to accompany them. The British officers involved were furious at the fiasco, and the enraged Sir George Brown was on the point of knocking down General d'Autemarre, the commander of the expedition's French troops.

A few days later, the encumbered and dispirited Canrobert presented the Emperor's plan for a fresh initiative in the Crimea to an allied Council of War. Coming in the aftermath of the Kertch fiasco it was not well received by the British, and Lord Raglan would not subscribe to it. Canrobert's endurance was now at an end and on 16 May he asked the Emperor to relieve him of the command of the French forces and give him instead a 'simple division' to lead. Canrobert's request was granted. He took over the 4th Division, while General Pélissier became French Commander-in-Chief.

Pélissier was a far more forthright and resolute man than Canrobert. His men called him 'tin head', and he called them 'a lot of bastards'. He was confident of his professional judgement, and not inclined to submit to directives from amateurs in Paris. As to matters in hand, he announced that he intended to give the Russians 'a sound thrashing' and would take speedy steps to capture the Mamelon.

On 22 May Pélissier gave double notice that he meant business when he authorised a savage night assault on the Russian defences

A panoramic view of the Sea of Azof, Kertch, Yenikale, Arabat.

between the Central Bastion and Quarantine Bay, and also gave permission for the Kertch expedition to go ahead. The night attack was terribly costly, the French losing 2,303 men (more than at Austerlitz), but it attained its object. The Kertch expedition was remarkably successful: Kertch and Yenikale were captured, a hundred guns taken, thousands of tons of corn and flour destroyed, Russian boats sunk, and depots and arsenals demolished; the Sea of Azof was laid open to Royal Navy gun boats which continued to wreak tremendous havoc in the area.

Three commanders: Lord Raglan, Omar Pasha and General Pélissier.

Pélissier's methods included the frank rejection of the Emperor's commands, and, once, the cutting of the irritating telegraph line. The French commander pressed ahead for a joint allied assault at the beginning of June which would result in the capture of the Mamelon. The Emperor objected to this plan, and informed Pélissier:

> For the welfare of France and for the glory of our arms you are at the head of the finest army which perhaps has ever existed. You are assured of an immortal reputation but it is necessary to do something great. The conduct of the siege comes closer to the qualifications of the general commanding the engineers [Niel] … If you want to continue the siege without surrounding the place you will only succeed after fierce and bloody struggles which will cost you your best troops … In accordance with the British Government which writes the same thing to Lord Raglan I order you positively not to persist at all with the siege

British guns, including naval guns, bombard Sebastopol.

> without having completely invested the place. You are then to consult with Lord Raglan and Omar Pasha to ensure the most effective offensive, be it by the Tchernaya or against Simpheropol. In laying out the course to follow we leave both of you the widest latitude on the means that you employ.

This unambiguous message was simply ignored by Pélissier until 8 June, when the Mamelon had been taken; then the French commander informed Napoleon III that the telegram had unfortunately been delayed. On 6 June the third bombardment of Sebastopol had taken place. Elegant British tourists watched the allied artillery pound the Mamelon, the White Works (which enfiladed the Malakov) and the Quarries (which guarded the approaches to the Redan). By 9 June, despite desperate Russian counter-attacks, the allies had achieved striking success: the

The Russians steadfastly defend Sebastopol.

French had swept on to the Mamelon, the British lay before the Redan.

Napoleon III, however, cabled Pélissier that 'I admire the courage of the troops but I would observe to you that a battle fought to decide the fate of the entire Crimea would not have cost you more. I persist then in the order which I had the Minister of War give you, to make all your efforts to enter resolutely into a field campaign.' In fury, Pélissier replied:

> Sire, in giving me the command ... Your majesty told me ... to conform as much as possible to a former plan which the English had clearly modified in their attacks. Everything has been done in accord with them and we have gone hand in hand. Our plans have been made clear to you and have succeeded ... My conviction is that this is the only path to follow. In this situation, the radical execution of your orders ... is impossible ... Your Majesty must free me from the narrow limits to which he had assigned me or else allow me to resign a command impossible to exercise in co-operation with our loyal allies at the somewhat paralysing end of an electric wire.

While Pélissier fumed and waited for a reply, the allies prepared for a major attack on the defences of Sebastopol. On 17 June the allied artillery once more pounded the Russian earthworks; it had been planned that on 18 June the British would capture the Redan, and the French the Malakov – which was generally regarded to be the key to the Russian defensive system.

After their successes of 8 and 9 June the allies were optimistic about the forthcoming attacks; as it happened they were both disastrous failures. There were several reasons for this. One was that the Russians had prior knowledge of the impending assault and had consequently prepared their positions well. A more important cause for failure lay in the actions of Pélissier himself: he had quarrelled with General Bosquet, who had studied the defences of the Malakov for several months, and had removed him from the command of the 2nd Corps; less excusably he altered the hour appointed for the joint attack to 3 am thus dispensing with the preliminary bombardment. Lord Raglan was not consulted over this latter decision, and simply had to conform to the new French plan. Consequently the British units had to be issued with a whole new set of orders, and, thereafter, confusion reigned.

Things were little better in the French army. Of the three French units that were to be launched against the Russian defences, one, under General Mayran, mistook the signal to attack and set off early at 2.50; in a desperate effort to rectify this error, Pélissier tried to get his other two units moving as well, but they were not ready to do so. All the French units faced a deadly fire when they eventually moved forward, and were cut to pieces by roundshot, canister, musket-balls and bullets. By 8.30 am Pélissier had pulled back his forces; the battle was over.

The British had fared equally badly. Determined to support the unfortunate French units, Lord Raglan sent in his men over a quarter of a mile of open ground. They struggled forward through a terrifying barrage of grape shot and musketry as if they were pressing into the face of some terrible tempest. It was an appalling defeat. Men fell on all sides: 1,500 British troops were lost, and Colonel Lacy Yea and General Sir John Campbell were among those killed. French losses were double those of the British; 1,500 dead and 1,600 wounded.

This humiliating reverse was a further, deadly, blow to Lord Raglan's spirits. For some weeks he had been downcast and exhausted, though, as usual, kind and considerate. The bitter attacks that were made upon him in the British press, and the failure of the allies to take Sebastopol, had taken their toll. On 14 June General Estcourt died of cholera, which was once again beginning to ravage the army. Lord Raglan became ill after Estcourt's funeral, which he had not dared to attend for fear of breaking down. He was exhausted, and suffered a violent attack of diarrhoea. Slowly his strength slipped from him, while he refused, gently and with his renowned courtesy, to accept the fact that he was dying.

On 28 June Lord Raglan died peacefully in his sleep. The army was shocked and grief-stricken by the unexpected death of the Commander-in-Chief; Canrobert and Pélissier mourned equally, the latter 'crying like a child ... for upwards of an hour' beside the death-bed. The body was shipped off to Bristol for a quiet burial at the family home at Badminton. Florence Nightingale was thunderstruck to hear of his death, and wrote, 'It was *not* cholera. The diarrhoea was slight but he was so *depressed* ... Peace be with him and his hecatomb of twenty thousand men.'

Lord Raglan's successor was not Sir George Brown who was already under medical orders to return home. Instead Sir James Simpson was confirmed in command of the army on 1 July. Simpson was a colourless nonentity, prostrated with gout, and with little military experience apart from the Peninsular War. He was soon oppressed by the difficulties that faced him.

One of the difficulties was that Omar Pasha, the Turkish commander, wanted to move his forces from the Crimea to protect the fortress of Kars, to the south-east of Trebizond in Asia Minor.

Sir James Simpson, who succeeded to the command of the British forces on Lord Raglan's death in June 1855.

Napoleon III was vehemently opposed to any such scheme and on 2 August 1855 sent the following memo to Marshal Vaillant, the French Minister for War:

> You must write to Pélissier: First, to consult always with General Simpson before undertaking anything; Second, to have better relations with Omar Pasha and try to use his troops; Third, to declare that the siege must be carried on; Fourth, to oppose any weakening of Ottoman forces in the Crimea. On this score, the English Government must perhaps hide the truth, but I know that in the French army it is said with a certain bitterness that the burden of the siege falls almost exclusively on us. We have sixty thousand at the siege, the English have twelve thousand! The Turks for whom we are fighting are never in the trenches, no more than the Sardinians. They say that it was Lord Raglan who hindered Canrobert [as well as] Pélissier from making a diversion which could have permitted investment of the fortress etc. etc. All this ought to be considered carefully. If now they still want to weaken the siege army by withdrawing Turkish troops they will create justified alienation in the French army. Furthermore the great objective now is at Sebastopol and not at Kars.

Lord Raglan's funeral, by William Simpson.

So the siege went on. On 16 August the Russian commander Gorchakov (who had earlier replaced Menshikov) launched an attack with four infantry divisions and two artillery brigades across the Chernaya river. The object was to recapture the Fediukine Heights, as a base for further operations against Balaclava and the Sapouné Heights. The Battle of the Chernaya ended in a decisive Russian defeat for which the French and Sardinian troops must take almost all the credit since only some British cavalry and artillery units took part. It was a significant event, however, since it represented the Russians' last effort to break the allied siege by operations in the field. Gorchakov, whose army had suffered over six thousand losses, sent a dispatch to the Minister of War in St Petersburg saying that it was mistaken to prolong the defence of Sebastopol.

General Simpson continued to be appalled by his responsibilities, and had, throughout July, written such pessimistic letters to Lord Panmure that the latter upbraided him on 28 July concluding

with the urgent advice 'But, my good friend, you must *lead*.' Simpson, however, was soon discussing his successor with Panmure, and concluding that General Sir William Codrington was the best choice (though Codrington did not take over until 11 November).

In the meantime, though little credit is due to Simpson, the long-besieged citadel fell on 8 September 1855. At 11.30 am a thunderous, intensive barrage opened up; forty minutes later, with bugles sounding and drums rattling, the Zouaves of General MacMahon's division spearheaded an assault on the Malakov;

Crimean gun emplacements. Note the protective fascines, wicker-work filled with earth or stones.

within ten minutes the tricolour was planted on the summit of the Malakov, which was held against fierce Russian counter-attack. The British assault on the Redan was conspicuously less successful: though the troops fought through to the foot of the Redan, they were pinned down, and the men refused to move from the cover of the parapet. After a few minutes they turned and fled back to their lines, leaving 2,500 comrades dead or wounded behind them. It was an inglorious conclusion to the siege, and the British Foreign Secretary, Lord Clarendon, wrote despairingly:

Removing the wounded from the Great Redan.

> Now I suppose the French will take it [the Great Redan] and will have a double crow over us, and we may expect heartburnings and recriminations. We have cut a poor figure lately and I expect we shall continue to do so as long as that worthy old gentle-woman, Simpson, is at the head of our affairs. I have a letter from Stratford [British Ambassador in Constantinople] today from headquarters saying that our army is living from hand to mouth and that we are even less prepared than last year for the winter while the French have vast stores of everything.

But even as the British licked their wounds, the Russians were preparing to abandon the town. During the night and the following morning great explosions made the earth shake as the enemy blew up magazines, barracks, arsenals and docks. After eleven months

Sebastopol had fallen, or rather, had been abandoned; but as the allies marched into the smoking ruins, Captain Henry Clifford noted ruefully 'I looked toward the Malakov, there was the French flag, the Tricolour, planted on its Parapet ... no flag floated on the Parapet on which I stood [the Redan] and if it had, I could have seized it and dashed it into the ditch we could not pass, or hid it in the bosom of the young officer, dead at my feet inside the Redan.'

Chapter 9

The War Outside the Crimea

The Royal Navy was the ideal weapon for prosecuting a wider war against Russia while the British army invaded the Crimea. A considerable part of the navy was of course sent to the Black Sea area where is supported the allied land forces, though Odessa, somewhat further afield, was bombarded in the early months of the war.

Twenty-seven Russian ships of the line, however, were at large in the Baltic Sea. In order to prevent this fleet from slipping out into the North Sea, and possibly menacing both the British coast and British shipping in the English Channel, the Admiralty gathered together a scratch force to contain the Russians within the Baltic Sea. The command of this hastily assembled fleet of sailing ships and steamers was given to the sixty-eight-year-old Sir Charles Napier. A member of a distinguished family of military men and administrators, Napier was known to his admirers as 'Fighting Charlie' and to the less enthusiastic as 'Dirty Charlie' on account of his unorthodox methods and sloppy dress; he was, however, a very competent commander.

Napier's task was not an easy one. He had to drum up naval recruits where he could find them – many were in fact army recruiting-sergeant's rejects – and train them as quickly as possible. Queen Victoria reviewed Napier's fleet at Portsmouth shortly before it set sail for the Baltic; at this ceremony Napier is reputed to have told the Queen that within a fortnight he would either be in Kronstadt (the Russian naval base in the Gulf of Finland) or in heaven! In fact, he was in neither place when two weeks had elapsed. There was little reason why he should have been: his ships were undermanned and short of ammunition, and Kronstadt was an extremely hard nut to crack, being well fortified and heavily garrisoned.

Opposite The British bombardment of the Baltic fortress of Sveaborg, August 1855, by Carl Glude.

Still, Napier sailed for the Baltic on 10 March 1854, eighteen days before Britain declared war on Russia. His fleet consisted of 4 screw-ships of the line, 4 blockships, 4 frigates and 3 paddle steamers, though other ships were to join later. With this diminutive force he was ordered by the Admiralty to seal the Baltic, to destroy the Russian fleet and to protect Danish and Swedish shipping and territory from Russian attack. Ranged against him were 27 Russian ships of the line, 10 frigates, 7 brigs, 9 steamers and many smaller gun boats.

The British fleet sailed first to Kiel, and from there to Köge Bay, south of Copenhagen. Napier considered this the best base from which to block the exits to the North Sea. Supplies were to

The naval war in the Baltic.

come from Flensburg which was on the end of a railway line built to Tonning by a Mr Peto, one of those bustling early-Victorian British businessmen that are so characteristic of the epoch. Mr Peto, in a further triumphant flourish of the glories of laissez faire capitalism, also put his fleet of steamers at the disposal of the British government!

Once supplied and securely based, how was the small British fleet to strike at the enemy to the greatest effect? The direct sea route to Russia lay through the two-hundred-mile long Gulf of Finland that led to St Petersburg, the Russian capital. The Gulf of Finland had four strong defensive points: Kronstadt, a formidably

Admiral Sir Charles Napier, first commander of Britain's Baltic Fleet.

fortified island barring the approaches to St Petersburg; the fortress of Sveaborg guarding the entrance to Helsingfors (Helsinki) – for Finland was a constitutionally governed Grand Duchy within the Russian Empire; Revel on the Esthonian coast, and Bomarsund, in the Aland Islands. There were secondary fortresses at Abö and Hangö in Finland.

On Napier's arrival in Copenhagen on 20 March 1854 he received information that the Russians were planning to take advantage of the early spring (the Gulf of Finland was ice-bound from December to April) by uniting their Sveaborg and Kronstadt squadrons.

Napier, however, spent over three weeks in Copenhagen (where it was noted that 'the Danes were excessively pleased with him for taking off his hat on landing'), training his crews in sailing techniques and (despite Admiralty parsimony over the use of shells) in gunnery. War, moreover, was not declared until 28 March, whereupon Napier was instructed to blockade the Gulf of Finland and any other convenient Russian ports, to intercept supplies from Finland to Aland, and to report on the possibility of attacking Bomarsund, Revel and other fortified ports.

As soon as he had received reports that Sveaborg was free of ice, and having ordered a reconnaissance of Bomarsund, Napier set off with his fleet from Copenhagen, arriving at the entrance to the Gulf of Finland on 17 April. There he ran into bad weather, and fog-bound and wind-swept, lacking local pilots, and with inefficient crews, he chose not to stay in such dangerous waters, and withdrew the fleet to Stockholm to await better weather. Once there he visited the King, in the hope of persuading him to come into the war on the side of the allies. The Swedish King listened patiently, but would not abandon his position of neutrality.

The weather improved during May and the fleet sailed to Hangö, where a few shots were exchanged with the garrison. In June the defences of Sveaborg were surveyed, and found to be too strong for any guns carried by the ships in the fleet. Admiral Plumridge was sent north to Aland and the Gulf of Bothnia with a squadron where he succeeded in inflicting much damage on Russian merchant ships and naval stores at Brahestad and Uleaborg. But at Tornea the expedition nearly came to grief when the landing party ran into a formidable force of Russian troops, and only escaped after suffering heavy casualties.

On 21 June, Captain Hall, whom Admiral Plumridge had left with three ships to watch Bomarsund, cashing in on the presence of a local pilot decided to attack Bomarsund on his own account. Anchoring out of range of the guns in the forts, he bombarded them for eight hours. Convinced that he had inflicted considerable damage, and having spent all his ammunition, he withdrew; but apart from setting fire to a few outbuildings, little was achieved except a prodigal waste of ammunition.

The allied fleet, now numbering twelve British and six French sail of the line, with nine steamers, set sail on 22 June for Kronstadt, leaving nine sail of the line and six frigates to watch Sveaborg. On 26 June, the fleet arrived off Kronstadt, near which was the Russian fleet of thirty ships, anchored in three columns. The allies spent three days in careful reconnaissance; as a result they discovered that the fortress, which contained many guns, could not be ap-

The Russian Baltic naval base of Kronstadt.

proached except by ships of shallow draught. Moreover it would be folly to attempt an attack with no special artillery, mortars or rockets, with eighteen capital ships against the Russians' twenty-two. Sir Charles Napier was, however, severely censured later for not attacking Kronstadt at this time, even though cholera had recently broken out among his men.

The allied ships withdrew from Kronstadt and sailed to Sveaborg, where Admiral Corry, with the squadron on watch, had made a detailed examination of the defences. He had discovered that Sveaborg was defended by booms, stakes, mines, and eight thousand troops in formidable fortifications made out of granite. Sir James Graham wrote from the Admiralty on 2 July to say that six thousand French troops, with ten guns, were to be sent in British ships for the Admiral to use either against Sveaborg or Bomarsund, though the Lords of the Admiralty preferred the latter. Napier replied that in his opinion Bomarsund would be the most suitable objective.

Bomarsund guarded the northern and most negotiable entrance to the great landlocked harbour of Aland, standing on a spit of land covering the narrow channel between the mainland and Prästo Island to the east. From the sea the spit was guarded by a semi-circular fort at water-level, holding 120 guns. On the landward side, the granite Forts Tzee and Nottich squatted on top of twin hills, guarding the approach from the flat ground behind the town. These great granite towers, with their bomb-proof iron roofs, boasted twenty-four guns each. On the landward side, however, the defences were not effective.

The military forces mustered for the attack consisted of some ten thousand French troops commanded by General D'Hilliers, and one thousand British, under Brigadier-General Jones of the Royal Engineers. The expedition embarked at Calais in ships of the Royal Navy and arrived off Aland early in August. On 8 August a landing

was made four miles north of Bomarsund; a contingent of British marines and sappers led the way, followed by a brigade of French marines. The main force of the French landed simultaneously south of Bomarsund. The forts were surrounded and batteries were placed in position to attack the round towers. By 13 August the allied guns were in position and the bombardment began.

Both forts were silenced, then reduced to ruins. The French stormed Fort Tzee on 14 August, and on the next day the British took Fort Nottich; the fleet bombarded the main fort and Prästo Island; Bomarsund was surrendered unconditionally soon after,

The Royal Navy attacks Bomarsund during the Baltic campaign, August 1854, by Hecla Valorous.

and its fortifications were destroyed. Although Aland was offered to Sweden as a diplomatic pawn, the offer was refused.

Napier now turned against Abö in Finland. A reconnaissance revealed the presence of seventeen gun boats, and a large force of infantry in the dense woods each side of the channel leading to the town. Sir Charles Napier was keen to attack, but General D'Hilliers refused to join the assault since many of his troops had cholera. The French were thus unlikely to attack Revel either, so Sir Charles turned instead to the possibility of capturing Sveaborg. General D'Hilliers and his chief engineer were taken to Sveaborg with Brigadier-General Jones. The French officers were convinced that there was nothing to be done so late in the year. The Brigadier, however, reported that an attack on the fortress could be made by landing guns on a nearby island from which the principal works in the dockyard could be destroyed. But on 4 September the French started to withdraw from the Baltic for the winter. Sir Charles Napier was ordered by the Admiralty to report on the possibilities of further action for the year, but by the time he received these orders, the French had already left for Cherbourg.

The Royal Navy kept up the blockade on the Russian coast until the end of October 1854, when the fleet was gradually withdrawn, first to Kiel and thence to Spithead, where, on 22 December, Napier was brusquely told 'you are hereby required and directed to strike your flag, and come on shore'.

This insulting directive was the culmination of a long series of disagreements between Napier and the Board of Admiralty. In fact, Napier had been strikingly successful: he had bottled up the Russian fleet in the Gulf of Finland; tied down an army of thirty thousand men; destroyed valuable ships and supplies, and captured Bomarsund. An acrimonious controversy ensued between Napier and the Admiralty, in which the former clearly demonstrated his lack of culpability. Finally, in atonement, the Admiralty offered Napier the GCB, the highest class of the Order of the Bath, which the admiral refused in a gesture of contempt.

In 1854 there were two other remarkable naval offensives against Russia. The first was a partial blockade of the White Sea in July by a small squadron of three British ships – *Eurydice*, a steamship of 26 guns, *Brisk*, a screw-corvette of 16 guns, and *Miranda*. This squadron sailed into the White Sea late in August, after bombarding Kola in northern Lapland; they proceeded to attack Solovetski Island in the Gulf of Onega, and boarded and examined over three hundred merchant vessels, seizing any that could be legitimately claimed as prizes.

The second venture saw a combined French and British force operating in the North Pacific. The allies attacked the Russian naval base at Petropaulovsk on the Kamchatka peninsula, but a landing by marines and seamen was beaten off with heavy casualties. The Admiral in command, Price, committed suicide just before the attack was launched, however, and this was hardly the best boost for the morale of the men involved.

In 1855 the Baltic naval war reopened with the warm waters of spring. In Napier's place was Admiral Dundas, who had been transferred from the Black Sea Fleet. Dundas had 19 screw and 1 sail ship of the line (which carried sixty guns), 14 frigates, 12 small steamers, 21 steam gunboats, and 15 mortar boats. To this the French contributed 3 ships of the line, 3 frigates and 10 other smaller gun boats. The fleet sailed in March, establishing once more the blockade of the Russian Baltic ports. In May reconnaissances were made to Revel, the Aland Islands, Hangö, Sveaborg and Kronstadt. But at Kronstadt the defences had been greatly strengthened during the winter, and an attack by large ships was still too difficult. A fleet consisting of more gun boats might have been more effective, but Dundas only had twenty.

Elsewhere the Royal Navy harried Russian shipping in the Gulf of Bothnia and at the mouth of the Gulf of Finland. The Russian forts at Svastholm and Frederiksham were destroyed. In August Sveaborg was subjected to a devastating bombardment

The allies bombard the Russian naval base of Sveaborg, which guarded the approach to Helsinki.

by Anglo-French vessels in which dockyards, stores, magazines and over twenty small ships were blown up and burnt. In November 1855 the fleet withdrew for the winter and further preparations, but the advent of peace meant that the campaign was not renewed.

In the Pacific, during 1855, two British squadrons (one under Admiral Bruce in the North Pacific and one under Admiral Stirling

in Chinese waters) were operating against the Russians, and a third squadron, under Commodore Elliot, was later assembled at Hong Kong. None of these forces, however, achieved much in the way of crippling the Russian war effort, since they found the enemy either too strong or too elusive to be dealt with effectively.

Apart from the naval war and the Crimean campaign the most

A triumphant Russian lithograph of 1855 entitled 'News from the Turkish frontier'.

important of the secondary operations against Russia took place in Asia Minor. From Batumi on the Black Sea to Ararat on the Persian border there were 150 miles of Turkish frontier with Russia. The main town in the region of what was then called Turkish Armenia was centred round the ancient fortress of Kars, eighty miles south-east of Batumi and approximately the same distance south-west of Tiflis. In the summer of 1854 a Russian army moved into Turkish Armenia, and on 29 July it attacked a Turkish division in front of Kars at a place called Bayezid. The Turks lost the battle and were driven back, losing a considerable amount of equipment. The Turkish commander at Kars, Zarif Mustapha Pasha, was determined to regain the initiative, and in August he attacked the Russians with an army of 22,000 Turkish infantry, 4,000 cavalry, 11,000 Bashi-Bazouks, 4,500 irregular cavalry and 52 guns. Prince Bebutov, the Russian commander who had failed to follow-up his success at Bayezid, had an army of 20,000 infantry, 5,000 of the renowned Cossacks, about 18,000 irregulars and 60 guns. Twenty miles east of Kars the two forces met. The battle lasted for five hours after which the Turks again fell back on Kars, having suffered about two thousand casualties and lost about another two thousand men as prisoners to the Russians. The Turks were defeated not so much because of the superior tactics of Prince Bebutov, but because Zarif Pasha was confused by the rival plans of his foreign advisers. But the Russians had also suffered heavy losses and once more failed to follow up their victory, thus affording the Turks another opportunity to recover. At this point the British army sent a gunner, Colonel Fenwick Williams, to Kars as Lord Raglan's liaison officer with Zarif Pasha. Williams had spent several years with the Turkish army and knew the Kars area well. He was accompanied by another gunner, Major Teasdale, as aide-de-camp, and also a Dr Sandwith who had been appointed Inspector-General of Hospitals in Asia Minor. At Constantinople, Williams had been told by Raglan that his duties were to report back to him on the organization and condition of the Turkish army in Armenia, and furthermore to establish good relations with any French military mission which might also be sent to the area.

Williams and his companion arrived in Kars in September 1854 (at approximately the same time as the Battle of Alma) and were met by General Guyon, an Irishman serving in the Ottoman army. Guyon told Williams of the appalling inefficiency and disastrously low state of morale in Kars. Accordingly Williams decided to take over himself. He struggled for months to improve the town's defences, requisitioned grain and supplies from the surrounding

Major-General
Sir William Fenwick
Williams, defender of
Kars, by W. Walker.

A Russian illustration showing the Turkish surrender at Kars in November 1855.

countryside, and settled down to withstand a Russian siege. The siege dragged on from June 1855 to November 1855 – in fact until after the fall of Sebastopol. Williams failed throughout to get relief and reinforcements from the Crimea where it was reckoned that the Turkish forces were needed to keep the Russians bottled up in Sebastopol and at bay in the countryside outside the town. Eventually the half-starved garrison at Kars was forced to capitulate on 25 November, despite the resolute defence offered to the Russian forces by the Turkish troops led and inspired by Colonel Williams.

In the fighting outside the Crimea, therefore, Britain demonstrated two of the strengths that made her such a remarkable power in the mid-nineteenth century: one was the daring and efficiency of her unbiquitous navy, and the other was the dogged and devoted service of single-minded men like Colonel Williams and his aides, who were prepared to adapt to a strange environment and outlandish conditions and (if possible) to mould them.

Chapter 10

The Peace

With the fall of Sebastopol the campaign in the Crimea petered out. There was no great clash of armies, though from time to time shots were exchanged. The scene of the most feverish activity and the most skilful stratagems was no longer the Crimean peninsula, nor even Asia Minor or the Baltic Sea; it was the conference room at Vienna, where the assembled delegates tried to hammer out the points of a peace settlement.

In the Crimea, the Russians proceeded to dig themselves in on the heights to the north of Sebastopol. The allied commanders were disinclined to attack them, because of the probable cost and the uncertain advantages to be gained from such an offensive. There were suggestions that some move might be made to cut the enemy's communications, possibly by sailing round to Eupatoria and moving south once more from there, or by pushing north-east into the peninsula, but nothing came of them. In any event, winter was closing in and soon brisk troop movements would be impossible; moreover, it was optimistically reckoned that when the privations of winter began, the Russians would be forced to abandon the Crimea.

The Emperor Napoleon III chafed at this inactivity, and continued to deluge Pélissier with directives and advice, most of which the French Commander-in-Chief ignored or robustly rebutted. One piece of Imperial advice was acted on, however; this was Napoleon's insistence that Kinburn should be occupied in order to block communication between Nicolaev, Kherson and Odessa, and to threaten the Russian Army's rear. General Bazaine undertook this operation with considerable success.

Opposite Delegates at the Congress of Paris 1856.

By November 1855, though the occasional roundshot whistled across Sebastopol harbour, the French were ready to conclude a peace. Napoleon sensed the mood of his nation and was prepared to accede to it, arguing that French losses had been heavier than the British and that the country could not afford a protracted war. Lord Palmerston, the British Prime Minister, expressed different views; he argued that the British army was about to reach a peak of strength and efficiency and was confident of doing really well in a spring campaign. He was backed up by the British public which was thirsting for the Russians to be soundly thrashed before the troops were brought home.

There were several reasons for the difference in attitude between the British and the French governments. Britain, with her possessions in India, and her commercial and colonial interests

General Sir William Codrington, who succeeded General Simpson as commander of British forces in the Crimea.

stretching from Gibraltar to Hong Kong, wanted Russia humbled and contained in the Eastern Mediterranean and the Near East. The French had no such far-flung interests. The Emperor wanted to achieve stability for his dynasty, and his immediate ambitions had been fulfilled by the fall of Sebastopol. His gaze was now turned on other quarters, and he began to dream of recreating another part of the Napoleonic legend by aiding European nationalist and liberal movements against autocratic tyranny; Italy began to occupy his thoughts, not Simferopol and Kars.

Thus France moved towards a *détente* with Russia, even while the allied commanders talked of ousting the enemy from the heights beyond Sebastopol and of sending forces to threaten them in Asia Minor. Nothing was done on this latter score, however, and the diplomats began to make substantial progress as 1856 opened.

In the Crimea, the faint-hearted General Simpson was succeeded in January by General Codrington. Plans were laid for the division of the allied forces into two armies, ready for spring campaigning: one led by Pélissier and composed of French, Sardinians and a few

British troops, to operate from Eupatoria; the other to be commanded by Codrington, and made up of British troops, mercenaries and some French, to operate from Sebastopol.

The winter of 1855–6 provided an odd contrast with the preceding one. The scandals of the first winter had at least resulted in sufficient reforms to guarantee the British troops a more comfortable experience during the second winter. As one observer put it, the British forces were now 'well-fed, well-clothed and well-sheltered ... [they] were a great contrast to those of the previous winter; no one would have taken the smart clean troops on the plateau of Sebastopol in January 1856 to have been of the same race and nation as the care-worn, over-worked, and sickly soldiers guarding the trenches in January 1855.' The French, by way of contrast, had a much worse winter than during 1854–5, due chiefly to widespread illness.

In February 1856, following a vigorous initiative by Austria, an armistice was arranged, to come into effect on 14 March. On 30 March the final peace treaty was signed in Paris. The Peace of Paris provided for the restoration to Russia of Sebastopol, Balaclava, Kamiesh, Eupatoria, Kertch, Kinburn and all other occupied areas; Kars was to be returned to Turkey. The Black Sea was to be neutralised: no naval bases or arsenals were to be maintained on its shores, and ships of war were denied access to or exit through the Bosphorus – though both Turkey and Russia were allowed to keep some light warships (the heaviest weighing eight hundred tons) in the Black Sea. The Danube was declared an open waterway. The Russians also ceded a small area of Southern Bessarabia which they had seized in 1828 – it was their only territorial concession. Turkish sovereignty in the Danubian principalities was to be guaranteed though the provinces were to be united as the new state of Romania; for his part, the Sultan declared that he was prepared to improve the conditions of all Christians within the Ottoman Empire. Ironically, there was no mention of the guardianship of the Holy Places – ostensibly the cause of the war.

Palmerston had throughout pressed for a hard treaty and had urged Lord Clarendon to hold out for tougher terms by reminding him that 'Faint Heart never won fair Lady.' There is no doubt that he was disappointed with the final treaty, though he presented it cheerfully enough to the Cabinet; but when the heralds proclaimed the peace terms in the City of London they were hissed, and the treaty was denounced in the House of Commons as being too soft.

The allies began to evacuate the Crimea as soon as the peace treaty was signed. Amid an almost festive atmosphere of sporting

Lord Clarendon, British Foreign Secretary at the peace negotiations.

events and military reviews, British, French and Russian troops fraternised. As the allies pulled out of their positions, Russian soldiers took their places. The last of the French forces left on 4 July, the last of the British on 12 July.

Despite the unpopularity of some of the peace terms, the British public welcomed the ending of the war; cannons were fired in the public parks and windows were illuminated. An estimated half a million people flocked into London to celebrate, and joined the two million Londoners already out for the festivities. Among the ephemera of the war were balaclava helmets, Crimean crocuses and Lindhal's *Alma, a Battlepiece for the Pianoforte*.

Had it all been worth it? Fourteen years later Russia denounced the treaty and reneged on its most significant clause – the neutrality of the Black Sea. A new Russian Black Sea Fleet was built, and in 1877 there was a new, terrifying 'Russian war scare' which was

Review of the Guards in Hyde Park after their return from the Crimea, July 1856.

only ended by the Treaty of Berlin a year later. Still, the integrity of the Turkish Empire had been maintained, and the ramshackle system survived until the enormous upheavals of the Great War.

For the British common soldier, who had achieved and endured so much, there were some short-term benefits. The national conscience was aroused by the endurance of the troops, and this stimulated a demand for military reform. But the impact of the Crimean War in this respect should not be exaggerated; reforms only trickled out for the rest of the Victorian age. Nor did the public reputation of the red-coated rank and file change for good overnight, and at the end of the century Kipling was writing ruefully of the plight of *Tommy*:

Yes, makin' mock o'uniforms that guard you while you sleep
Is cheaper than them uniforms, an' they're starvation cheap;
An' hustlin' drunken soldiers when they're goin' large a bit

Lord Cardigan explaining the triumphs and trials of the war to his family.

Is five times better business than paradin' in full kit.
Then it's Tommy this, an' Tommy that, an' "Tommy 'ow's yer soul?"
But it's "Thin red line of 'eroes" when the drums begin to roll –
The drums begin to roll, my boys, the drums begin to roll.
O it's "Thin red line of 'eroes" when the drums begin to roll.

Nor were the officers, who had demonstrated their bravery and spontaneity as well as their lack of professionalism in the Crimea, transformed at a stroke into first-rate tacticians and sound strategists. The Victorian officer class remained blue-blooded and, at times, distinctly bone-headed – as a variety of campaigns from India to Zululand, and from Afghanistan to South Africa demonstrate. Indeed, if the Victorian age is still popularly associated with 'progress', an analysis of the fortunes of the British army from the Crimean War to the death of the Old Queen in 1901 will do much to dispel the illusion.

Appendix 1

Order of battle at the Alma, 20 September 1854

I. BRITISH ARMY (one battalion from each of the regiments named below)
Commander-in-Chief: Field-Marshal Lord Raglan (the Hon. Fitzroy James Henry Somerset)

Front Line:

- *2nd Division* (Lieutenant-General Sir George De Lacy Evans) — 5000 infantry
  - Right brigade:
    (Brigadier-General Adams)
    - 41st Regiment
    - 49th Regiment
    - 47th Regiment
  - Left brigade:
    (Brigadier-General Pennefather)
    - 30th Regiment
    - 55th Regiment
    - 95th Regiment
  - [5000 infantry]
- *Light Division* (Lieutenant-General Sir George Brown)
  - Right brigade:
    (Brigadier-General Codrington)
    - 7th Regiment
    - 33rd Regiment
    - 23rd Regiment
  - Left brigade:
    (Brigadier-General Buller)
    - 19th Regiment
    - 88th Regiment
    - 77th Regiment
  - [5000 infantry]

Second Line:

- *1st Division* (Lieutenant-General His Royal Highness the Duke of Cambridge)
  - Right brigade:
    (Brigadier-General Bentinck)
    - Grenadier Guards
    - Scots Fusiliers
    - Coldstream Guards
    - [the Brigade of Guards]
  - Left brigade:
    (Brigadier-General Sir Colin Campbell)
    - Royal Highland Regiment 42nd (The Black Watch)
    - 93rd Argyll & Sutherland Highlanders
    - 79th Queen's Own Cameron Highlanders
    - [the Highland Brigade]
  - [5000 infantry]

Reserve:

3rd Division (Major-General Sir Richard England)

Right brigade:

(Brigadier-General Sir J. Campbell)

1st, 4th, 28th, 38th Regiments

Left brigade:

(Brigadier Sir W. Eyre)

44th, 50th, 60th, 68th Regiments

4th Division (Major-General Sir George Cathcart)

Right brigade:

20th, 21st, 63rd Regiments

Left brigade:

46th, 56th Regiments, 1st Rifle Brigade

Cavalry: (Major-General Lord Lucan and Brigadier-General Lord Cardigan)

4th and 13th Light Dragoons

8th, 11th and 17th Hussars

Artillery:

8 batteries field artillery (64 guns)

1 troop horse artillery (4 guns)

2. FRENCH ARMY

Commander-in-Chief: Marshal Armand Jacques Leroy de St Arnaud

1st Division: General François Certain Canrobert

2nd Division: General Pierre François Joseph Bosquet

3rd Division: General Prince Jerome Charles Napoleon

4th Division: General Élie Frédéric Forey

8½ batteries field artillery (68 guns)

9,000 Turks

Army HQ (St Arnaud) Chief of Staff, de Martimprey; ADC Trochu

1st Division (Canrobert)

1st Brigade (Espinasse)

4th Chasseurs

1st Zouaves

7th de Ligne

2nd Brigade (Vinoy)

9th Chasseurs

20th de Ligne

27th de Ligne

2nd Division (Bosquet)

1st Brigade (D'Autemarre)

Tirailleurs

3rd Zouaves

50th de Ligne

2nd Brigade (Bouat)

3rd Chasseurs

7th Léger

6th de Ligne

3rd Division (Prince Napoleon)

1st Brigade (Monet)

2nd Zouaves

Marine Regiment

2nd Brigade (Thomas)

22nd Léger

4th Division (Forey)
1st Brigade (de Lourmel)
5th Chasseurs
19th, 26th de Ligne
2nd Brigade (Aurelle)
39th, 74th de Ligne
Cavalry Brigade (D'Allonville)
1st Chasseurs d'Afrique
4th Chasseurs d'Afrique
Cavalry Brigade (Cassaignolles)
6th Dragoons
6th Cuirassiers
Chief Engineer (Bizot)

3. RUSSIAN ARMY

Army HQ (Prince Menshikov)
16th Division (Kvetinski)
1st Brigade
Vladimir Regiment
Susdal Regiment
2nd Brigade
Uglitz Regiment
Kazan Regiment
16th Artillery Brigade
2 light batteries
1 heavy battery
17th Division (Kiriakov)
1st Brigade
Moscow Regiment
2nd Brigade
Borodino Regiment
Tarutin Regiment
17th Artillery Brigade
2 light batteries
1 heavy battery
14th Division (Gorchakov)
1st Brigade
Volhynia Regiment
Minsk Regiment
Additional troops
6th Rifle Battalion
4 reserve bns Brest–Bialystok Regt (from 13th Div)
2 battalions sailors, with 4 guns
Cavalry
2 Sqdns Hussars (outpost line)
2 Sqdns Cossacks
2 Regiments Hussars
2 Regiments Don Cossacks
2 Horse Artillery batteries

Appendix 2

The bombardment of Sebastopol, 17 October 1854

The allied fleets took up positions near the harbour entrance and the British fleet came into action in the following order:

	Ship	*Guns*	*Commanded by*	*Towed by*
1.	*Albion*	90	Captain Stephen Lushington	*Firebrand*
2.	*Arethusa*	50	Captain Symonds	*Triton*
3.	*London*	90	Captain Charles Eden	*Niger*
4.	*Sanspareil*	70	Captain Dacres	
5.	*Agamemnon*		Admiral Lord Lyons Captain Mends	
6.	*Rodney*	90	Captain G. Graham	*Spiteful*
7.	*Bellerophon*	78	Captain Lord George Paulet	*Cyclops*
8.	*Queen*	116	Captain Mitchell	*Vesuvius*
9.	*Vengeance*	84	Captain Lord Edward Russell	*Highflyer*
10.	*Trafalgar*	120	Captain Greville	*Retribution*
11.	*Britannia*	120	Admiral Sir J. D. Dundas Captain Carleton	*Furious*

Each of the ships was towed into action by a steamer lashed along the port side.

The following are the names of the French line-of-battle ships which followed the British fleet into action. (The French moved in two columns; *Jupiter* leading the port column, *Napoleon* the starboard column.)

	Ship	*Guns*		*Ship*	*Guns*
1.	*Jupiter*	82	8.	*Napoleon*	90
2.	*Bayard*	82	9.	*Henry IV*	100
3.	*Suffren*	82	10.	*Valmy*	114
4.	*Ville de Marseilles*	70	11.	*Ville de Paris*	114
5.	*Marengo*	70	12.	*Friedland*	114
6.	*Jean Bait*	80	13.	*Morte Bello*	114
7.	*Algiers*	70	14.	*Charlemagne*	80

Appendix 3

Order of battle before Inkerman, 5 November 1854

1. BRITISH

Cavalry (Earl of Lucan)
Heavy Brigade (Scarlett)
4th and 5th Dragoon Guards
1st and 2nd Dragoons
6th Inniskilling Dragoons
Light Brigade (Cardigan)
4th Light Dragoons
8th and 11th Hussars
13th Light Dragoons
17th Lancers

Infantry
1st Division (H.R.H. the Duke of Cambridge)
Guards Brigade (Bentinck)
3rd Battalion Grenadier Guards
1st Battalion Coldstream Guards
1st Battalion Scots Fusilier Guards
Highland Brigade (C. Campbell)
42nd, 79th, and 93rd
2nd Division (Evans)
1st Brigade (Adams)
41st, 47th, and 49th
2nd Brigade (Pennefather)
30th, 55th, and 95th
3rd Division (England)
1st Brigade (Campbell)
1st Royals, 38th, and 50th
2nd Brigade (Eyre)
4th, 28th, and 44th
4th Division (Cathcart)
1st Brigade (Goldie)
20th, 21st, 57th, and 68th
2nd Brigade (Torrens)
63rd
1st Battalion Rifle Brigade
46th, 2 Companies
Light Division (Brown)
1st Brigade (Codrington)
7th, 23rd, and 33rd
2nd Brigade (Buller)
19th, 77th, 88th
2nd Battalion Rifle Brigade

Artillery

7 batteries, and two 18-pounders, with the divisions on the plateau

2 troops (Captains Maude and Brandling) and 1 battery (Barker) at or near Balaclava.

Engineers

3rd, 4th, 8th, 10th and 11th Companies

Total strength in the five British infantry divisions about 22,000 men.

2. RUSSIAN

SOIMONOV'S ARMY (19,000 men, 38 guns)

10th Division

1st Brigade

Katerinburg Regiment

2nd Brigade

Tomsk Regiment

Koliwan Regiment

16th Division

1st Brigade

Vladimir Regiment

Susdal Regiment

2nd Brigade

Uglitz Regiment

17th Division

1st Brigade

Butirsk Regiment

PAULOV'S ARMY (16,000 men, 96 guns)

11th Division

1st Brigade

Selinghinsk Regiment

Yakutsk Regiment

2nd Brigade

Okhotsk Regiment

17th Division

2nd Brigade

Borodino Regiment

Tarutin Regiment

GORCHAKOV'S ARMY (Balaclava front) 20,000 men, 88 guns

Appendix 4

British artillery in the Crimea

FIELD ARTILLERY

Weight of shell	*Calibre*	*Overall weight behind Gun teams*	*maximum range*
6 pr	3·6″	27 cwt	600 yds
9 pr	4·2″	38 cwt	800 yds
12 pr howitzer	4·5″	29 cwt	1000 yds
24 pr ,,	5·7″	38 cwt	1025 yds

Types of ammunition used – shot, common shell, shrapnel (up to maximum range); case shot and carcasses (incendiaries) (range up to about 350 yards).

CONGREVE ROCKETS

6 pr			600 yds
12 pr			1000 yds

POSITION ARTILLERY

12 pr	4·6″	44 cwt	1000 yds
18 pr	5·2″	65 cwt	2000 yds
32 pr howitzer	6·3″	46 cwt	1400 yds
8 inch ,,	8″	54 cwt	1700 yds

SIEGE ARTILLERY

8″ and 10″ guns and howitzers			2000 yds
32 pr			2900 yds
68 pr			2600 yds
Lancaster gun			

MORTARS

8″			1720 yds
10″			2530 yds
13″			2700 yds

Mortars were fired at a fixed elevation of 45°, the range being varied by altering the charge. Once the range was found, they could be fired repeatedly without being relaid. For this reason they were mainly kept for night firing, while the day bombardment was carried out by the 'horizontal fire' of the guns.

Appendix 5

Casualties

British forces suffered 18,058 fatalities in the Crimean War. Of these casualties only 1761 were killed by enemy action, the rest died of wounds or (much more commonly) of disease. The vast majority of the 16,297 who died through the latter causes were stricken during the first nine months of the campaign when the mortality rate in some units reached a horrifying 60 per cent.

Select Calendar of Events

1853		
March	2	Menshikov arrives in Constantinople with demands on the Porte.
May	21	Menshikov leaves Constantinople, breaking off relations.
	31	Russian ultimatum to Turkey.
June	8	British Fleet approaches Dardanelles.
July	3	Russian army crosses the Pruth into Moldavia.
Oct	5	Turkey declares war on Russia.
	28	Turkish army crosses the Danube at Kalafat.
	30	British Fleet enters the Bosphorus.
Nov	4	Russians defeated by Turks at Oltenitza.
	30	Turkish naval squadron destroyed at Sinope.
1854		
Jan	4	Allied fleets enter the Black Sea.
	8	Russians invade the Dobruja.
Feb	23	The Guards leave England.
March	10	Baltic Fleet leaves Spithead.
	19	French troops sail for Turkey.
	20	French Baltic Fleet sails.
	28	France and Great Britain declare war on Russia.
April	5	British arrive at Gallipoli.
	14	Russians besiege Silistria.
	18	Turkish victory at Rahova.
	20	Austria and Prussia declare their neutrality.
	22	Bombardment of Odessa.
May	28	Embarkation of Allied force for Varna.
June	23	Russians abandon the siege of Silistria.
	26	Allied fleet arrives off Kronstadt.
July	7	Russians defeated at Giurgevo.
	28	Russians withdraw across Pruth.
	28	Russians defeat Turks at Bayezid in Asia Minor.
Aug	13	Allies besiege Bomarsund.
	16	Surrender of Bomarsund.

Aug	21	Bombardment of Kola, in the White Sea, by British squadron.
	30	British naval failure at Petropaulovsk.
Sept	5	Allies embark at Varna for Crimea.
	14	Landing at Calamita Bay.
	19	Encounter at River Bulganek.
	20	Battle of Alma.
	23	Russian fleet scuttled in Sebastopol.
	24	Arrival of Col Williams at Kars.
		'Flank march' of the allies round Sebastopol.
	26	British arrive at Balaclava.
	29	Death of St Arnaud.
Oct	12	*Times* Fund set up.
	13	Patriotic Fund set up.
	17	First Bombardment of Sebastopol.
	23	Departure of Florence Nightingale and 38 nurses from England.
	25	Battle of Balaclava.
	26	Russian attack of 'Little Inkerman'.
Nov	5	Battle of Inkerman.
		Florence Nightingale arrives at Scutari.
	14	Hurricane in Crimea.
Dec	22	Sir Edmund Lyons replaces Admiral Dundas as commander of British Fleet.
	24	Admiral Bruat succeeds Admiral Hamelin in command of French Fleet.

1855

Jan	10	Russian feint attack on Balaclava.
	17	Russian attack on Eupatoria.
	26	Sardinia joins the Allies.
	31	Fall of Lord Aberdeen's government.
Feb	5	Lord Palmerston forms new government.
	20	Allied attack across Chernaya frustrated by snowstorm.
	22	Russians seize and fortify the Mamelon.
	24	French attack on 'White Works' defeated.
March	2	Death of Tsar Nicholas I, succession of Alexander II, who recalls Menshikov.
	15	Vienna conference opens.
April	4	Second Baltic expedition leaves Spithead.
	9	Second Bombardment of Sebastopol.
	26	Vienna conference closes.

May	1	Fierce fighting on the French left, at the Quarantine Cemetery.
	2	First expedition sails for Kertch and is recalled by Canrobert.
	16	Canrobert resigns command of French army and is succeeded by Pélissier.
	23	Expedition to Kertch sails again.
	25	Capture of Kertch and Yenikale.
	26	Allied naval forces enter Sea of Azof.
June	5	'Massacre' of boats' crew at Hangö.
	6	Third Bombardment of Sebastopol.
	8 & 9	Capture of the 'White Works', the Mamelon and The Quarries by the Allies.
	16	First Russian attack at Kars.
	17	Fourth Bombardment of Sebastopol.
	18	Main assault on the Malakov and Redan defeated with heavy loss.
	28	Death of Lord Raglan.
July	1	General Sir James Simpson appointed to command British army.
	14	Conference at which Omar Pasha asks permission to withdraw troops for Asia Minor.
Aug	7	Second Russian attack at Kars.
	9	Bombardment of Sveaborg.
	16	Russian attack at Battle of Chernaya defeated by French and Sardinian forces.
	17	Fifth Bombardment of Sebastopol.
Sept	5	Sixth Bombardment of Sebastopol.
	6	Omar Pasha leaves for Asia Minor.
	8	Attack on Malakov by French is successful, though French fail at Little Redan and Bastion du Mât.
		British fail at the Redan.
	9	Russians evacuate Sebastopol.
	29	Russian attack at Kars defeated.
		Cavalry skirmishing at Eupatoria.
		Omar Pasha's troops embark for Asia Minor.
Oct	3	Omar Pasha lands at Suchum Kaleh, with expedition for relief of Kars.
	7	Kinburn expedition sails.
	17	Allied expedition captures Kinburn, Ochakov evacuated.
	22	Selim Pasha's army lands at Trebizond and marches to Erzerum.

Nov	6	Omar Pasha defeats Russians on River Ingur.
	11	Sir James Simpson resigns, succeeded by Sir William Codrington.
	15	French magazine at Sebastopol explodes.
	25	Surrender of Kars.
Dec	8	Omar Pasha's army forced to withdraw from River Skeniscal.

1856

Jan	16	The Tsar accepts the Austrian demands.
	29	Russian guns bombard Sebastopol.
Feb	24	Paris Peace Conference opens.
	29	Armistice in the Crimea.
March	30	Treaty of Paris signed.
April	27	Ratification of Treaty of Paris, formal end of the war.

Select Bibliography

Barker, A. J., *The Vainglorious War 1854–6*, London, 1970

Blake, ffrench, R. L. V., *The Crimean War*, London, 1971

Brackenbury, G., *The Campaign in the Crimea* (2 vols.), London, 1855–6

Cardigan, Earl of, *Eight Months on Active Service*, London, 1856

Clifford, Henry, *Henry Clifford, VC His Letters and Sketches from the Crimea*, Toronto, 1956

Duberly, Frances Isabella, *Journal Kept During the Russian War*, London, 1855 and 1963

Gibbs, P., *Crimean Blunder*, London, 1960

Gooch, B. D., *The New Bonapartist Generals in the Crimean War*, The Hague, 1959

Hibbert, Christopher, *The Destruction of Lord Raglan*, London, 1961

Hume, S. R., *Reminiscences of the Crimean Campaign*, London, 1894

Judd, Denis, *Someone Has Blundered*, London, 1973

Kinglake, A. W., *The Invasion of the Crimea* (8 vols.), London, 1863–87

Nolan, E. H., *The History of the War Against Russia* (2 vols.), London, 1857

Reid, A. D., *Memories of the Crimean War*, London, 1911

Russell, W. H., *Complete History of the Crimean War*, New York, 1856

Russell, W. H., *The British Expedition to the Crimea*, London, 1858

Sandwith, H., *A Narrative of the Siege of Kars*, London, 1856

Selby, J. M., *The Thin Red Line*, London, 1970

Sterling, A. C., *The Highland Brigade in the Crimea*, London, 1895

Warner, P., *The Crimean War*, London, 1972

Wood, Sir Evelyn, *The Crimea in 1854 and 1894*, London, 1895

Woodham-Smith, C., *Florence Nightingale*, London, 1950

Woodham-Smith, C., *The Reason Why*, London, 1953

Index